OECD Reviews of Risk Management Policies

Assessing the Real Cost of Disasters

THE NEED FOR BETTER EVIDENCE

This work is published under the responsibility of the Secretary-General of the OECD. The opinions expressed and arguments employed herein do not necessarily reflect the official views of OECD member countries.

This document, as well as any data and any map included herein, are without prejudice to the status of or sovereignty over any territory, to the delimitation of international frontiers and boundaries and to the name of any territory, city or area.

Please cite this publication as:
OECD (2018), *Assessing the Real Cost of Disasters: The Need for Better Evidence*, OECD Reviews of Risk Management Policies, OECD Publishing, Paris.
http://dx.doi.org/10.1787/9789264298798-en

ISBN 978-92-64-29873-6 (print)
ISBN 978-92-64-29879-8 (PDF)

Series: OECD Reviews of Risk Management Policies
ISSN 1993-4092 (print)
ISSN 1993-4106 (online)

The statistical data for Israel are supplied by and under the responsibility of the relevant Israeli authorities. The use of such data by the OECD is without prejudice to the status of the Golan Heights, East Jerusalem and Israeli settlements in the West Bank under the terms of international law.

Photo credits: Cover ©Tzachi Tessler

Corrigenda to OECD publications may be found on line at: *www.oecd.org/about/publishing/corrigenda.htm*.

Foreword

Disasters cost lives and disrupt socio-economic activities and livelihoods, causing important economic costs each time they occur. Major earthquakes in Chile, Italy, Japan and Mexico; the disastrous 2017 hurricane season in the United States and the Caribbean; and wildfires in Canada, Portugal and Greece have all left devastation in their wake. Meanwhile, governments continue to invest in disaster risk management, building dikes, sea barriers and dams, strengthening regulations for building codes and land use, and communicating risks to stakeholders. To ensure that disaster risk management policies are effective and address the right priorities, policy makers need solid evidence on damages avoided as well as on resources already engaged in managing disaster risks.

How much do countries know about the real cost of disasters? This book provides an overview of OECD countries' efforts to collect information on both the economic impacts of disasters and the level of public resources invested in the management of risk. It is based on the results of an OECD survey, two expert meetings held in 2014 and 2016 as well as complementary research conducted by the OECD Secretariat.

This report shows that, in many countries, data on the economic impact of disasters are sparse, especially for smaller-scale disasters. Where data are available, it is often not clear to what extent the estimates include both disaster damages (direct economic impacts) and losses (indirect economic impacts). Often, assessments rely on information on insured losses, which does not necessarily capture the full economic impact of a disaster. Few countries examine the distributional impacts of disasters, which are particularly relevant for effective disaster assistance programmes. In many countries, data on the public resources engaged in disaster risk management are similarly hard to come by. International efforts, such as the Sendai Framework for Disaster Risk Reduction Monitoring Process, are starting to slowly bear fruit, but further investment will be needed to build a comprehensive evidence base on the cost of disasters.

This report was prepared with the support of the Public Governance Directorate under the auspices of the OECD's High Level Risk Forum, which promotes an integrated, whole-of-government approach to risk management and governance. The Forum brings together policy makers from governments, practitioners from the private sector and civil society, and experts from think tanks and academia to identify and share good practices and deepen their understanding of risk management. The work of the Forum is underpinned by the Recommendation of the OECD Council on the Governance of Critical Risks. The findings presented in this report will be of interest to international discussions on the impact of disasters and on creating broader conditions for economic and social resilience, including through the post-2015 Sustainable Development Goals.

Acknowledgements

This report was prepared under the auspices of the OECD High Level Risk Forum by the OECD Public Governance Directorate, led by Marcos Bonturi.

The report presents the results of the work of OECD High Level Risk Forum to improve the evidence base on the costs of disasters by assessing countries progress, challenges and good practices. This report was co-ordinated and written by Cathérine Désirée Gamper. Stéphane Jacobzone, Deputy Head of the Reform of the Public Sector Division, and Jack Radisch, Senior Project Manager, supervised the work. Valuable research assistance throughout the project was provided by Melissa Li, James Drummond, Roberto Schiano Lomoriello and Teresa Maria Deubelli, who also contributed to writing the synthesis and chapters.

The Secretariat gratefully acknowledges the continued support for this activity by Japan, through the Ministry of Land, Infrastructure, Transport and Tourism (MLIT) and the Japan Institute of Country-ology and Engineering (JICE). The Secretariat is grateful to Mr. Tomoyuki Okada, Dr. Kenzo Hiroki, Mr. Yusuke Amano and Mr. Kenichiro Tachi (MLIT) and Dr. Masato Okabe (JICE) for their valuable contributions and feedback over the years and to this report in particular.

The Secretariat is grateful for comments and suggestions on earlier versions of this work received from Stephane Hallegatte (World Bank), Tom de Groeve (Joint Research Centre of the European Commission), Prof. Reimund Schwarze (Helmholtz Centre for Environmental Research), Prof. Debarati Guha-Sapir (University of Louvain/CRED), Dr. Reinhard Mechler and Thomas Schinko (International Institute for Applied Systems Analysis). Mr. Tomoyuki Okada (MLIT) provided valuable comments on the final version of the report.

The report benefited from discussions held at the 2016 Joint Expert Meeting on Disaster Loss Data, organised by the OECD and the European Commission Joint Research Centre (JRC) together with Horizon 2020 Platform for Climate Adaptation and Risk Reduction (PLACARD). Special thanks go to the speakers and experts involved in the process for all their valuable insights.

Liv Gaunt, Andrea Uhrhammer and Stéphanie Lincourt prepared the report for publication. The team is very grateful for assistance provided by Elisabeth Huggard and Susan Rantalainen throughout the project.

Table of contents

Tables

Figures

Boxes

Executive Summary

Beyond the human costs, disasters continue to cause significant disruptions to socio-economic activities. The extent of these disruptions is a major policy concern. However, the data needed to fully account for these shocks remain incomplete. The most comprehensive international repositories of information on past disasters contain data on the economic impact of less than half of the recorded disaster events. The information that is available is often gathered from diverse sources with different aims. Furthermore, there is no standard methodology for assessing disasters' economic impacts. Some databases collect information on disaster damages and losses due to business disruptions; others include only data on insured losses, while still others only include disaster damages over a certain threshold . This makes comparison between events within and across countries difficult.

Despite the challenges faced, policies for disaster risk management can only be effective if they are grounded in solid evidence. Governments need to make convincing arguments for allocating resources to measures that reduce future disaster risk. Projections and probabilistic modelling can, to some extent, inform the calculation of likely future economic impacts, but the accuracy of such models would be greatly enhanced by information on the actual impacts of past disasters.

Therefore, there is a need to increase data collection both on the economic impact of disasters as well as on the expenditure that is incurred in disaster risk management. Knowing how much is spent on managing the consequences of disasters helps policy makers better understand the longer-term effectiveness of disaster risk reduction measures. It is equally important to increase the sharing of such information across countries, given the uneven frequency of major events and the difficulty of co-ordinating responses.

This report examines the current efforts of OECD countries to collect this information.

Key findings

- *The larger a disaster is, the better the records are on its economic impacts.* Even though countries increasingly gather information on damages from major disasters, few have established national repositories for storing this information. However, when a significant disaster occurs, the majority of countries gather information on damages systematically, using established methods. For smaller hazardous events, data is less readily available.
- *The information labelled as "economic impact" may not actually be as comprehensive as the term suggests.* Country records show that it is not clear to what extent such information includes both disaster damages (direct economic impacts) and losses due to disruption (indirect economic impacts). Often, it is also not clear what exactly is registered within these categories. Most often, economic impact assessments use only insured loss information as the best available estimate, or only reflect damages to some, but not all, asset categories (e.g. only damages to public assets).

- *The distributional impacts of disasters are not systematically examined.* Differentiating disaster losses according to the type or group of actors that incurred them, such as low-income households or small businesses, can greatly enhance the effectiveness of a government's post-disaster financial assistance. Such information can also help governments tailor longer-term risk reduction strategies to different target groups. Most countries do not currently collect such differentiated economic impact data. However, there are a number of existing practices that could be adjusted to include information on distributional impacts in disaster loss data.
- *Formal requirements to establish disaster loss and damage information repositories are useful, but not always necessary.* For example, the storm Xynthia that hit France in 2011 led to the establishment of a national disaster loss data repository hosted by the French Observatory of Natural Risks.
- *The more fragmented the responsibilities for disaster risk management, the more scattered the existing disaster impact information.* In countries where different agencies and ministries are responsible for managing different types of risks, disaster damage data is often collected and stored in separate repositories. This can make it difficult to implement an integrated national disaster risk management policy.
- *In most countries, little consolidated information is available on disaster risk management expenditure.* Where such information exists, it is rarely gathered on a regular basis and it requires a special research effort to collect it. Accounting systems that do not include such information, as well as administrative fragmentation across sectors and levels of government impede easy and systematic access to this important information.
- *Increased international efforts to enhance information on the costs of disasters are starting to produce results.* Processes such as the Sendai Framework for Disaster Risk Reduction and the Sustainable Development Goals have spurred countries to improve their disaster cost records. Regional efforts, such as those in Europe and Asia, have also helped. It will be important to monitor the implementation of these renewed commitments to collect disaster cost data in a co-ordinated manner, so as to ensure comparability across datasets.

Introduction

Most OECD countries are periodically exposed to intense natural hazards, as well as man-made threats. A recent OECD-wide survey on the Governance of Critical Risks[1] showed that sudden on-set natural hazards, such as storms, floods, forest fires and earthquakes are considered a critical risk in more countries than other types of risks, such as man-made hazards (e.g. industrial accidents, cyber-attacks and terrorism). Despite concerted efforts in disaster risk reduction across OECD countries, major disasters continue to cause significant disruptions to socio-economic activities.

The extent of these socio-economic disruptions on the local and national levels remains unclear, since the available data on economic costs is often incomplete. EM-DAT, one of the few more comprehensive international disaster databases, for example, only includes economic cost data for slightly less than half of the disaster entries registered for OECD countries. Countries have made progress in establishing institutional arrangements to collect data on disaster-related economic costs, but methods of measurement differ greatly across countries as well as the comprehensiveness of data collected from one event to another. These differences result in a scattered, far from complete picture that obscures comparability across countries. The focus of data collection related to economic impacts continues to be on damages[2] caused by disasters. Only a few OECD countries measure losses[3], such as the costs associated with business interruption.

Policy-makers need to make convincing arguments in their resource allocation requests that disaster risk management (DRM) activities are cost effective. This includes showing that investments in disaster risk reduction are effectively reducing socio-economic costs. A systematic recording of how much is spent on managing the consequences of disasters helps to understand the longer term benefits of investments to reduce disaster damages and losses. Only a few OECD countries systematically track public expenditure for DRM. In most countries there is currently no central repository that clearly distinguishes and accounts for expenditures on disaster risk management. Due to the administrative set-up of many countries this information is dispersed across multiple agencies at different levels of government. In the few cases where such information is collected and centralised, the methods to measure it differ vastly, e.g. physical infrastructure investments are generally included, but non-structural investments in disaster risk reduction are often not accounted for. As a consequence, policy makers in many OECD countries have to rely on an incomplete picture of their country's spending on disaster risk management.

This report presents and discusses the results of research conducted under the auspices of the OECD High Level Risk Forum to assess and improve countries' measurement of disaster damages and losses as well as the availability of information on disaster risk management expenditures. The findings presented in this report have been used to support discussions and reflect on the conclusions and results of the Open-ended Intergovernmental Expert Working Group (OEIWG) on indicators[4], established by the

UN General Assembly as part of the implementation process for the Sendai Framework for Disaster Risk Reduction 2015 – 2030 (hereafter the "Sendai Framework").

The report examines the efforts OECD countries have undertaken to collect information on disaster damages and losses and disaster risk management expenditures based on information made available through the 2016 OECD survey on the "Cost of Disasters"[5]; (ii) two OECD expert workshops held in 2014 and 2016 on the "Cost of Disasters"; and (iii) additional desk research carried out by the OECD Secretariat.

Chapter 1 describes the rationale for improving the evidence base on the cost of disasters and provides a synthesis discussion of the research results concerning what countries have done to measure the costs of disasters. It also includes a brief discussion on how countries' current measurement practices compare to the standards agreed by the international community as part of the Sendai Framework for Disaster Risk Reduction as well as the Sustainable Development Goals.

Chapter 2 presents and summarises the detailed findings of the OECD's survey of countries' approaches and progress in measuring the damages and losses caused by disasters.

Chapter 3 gives an overview over country practices in the recording of disaster risk management expenditures.

Chapters 2 and 3 build on the results of the OECD surveys that were carried out as part of the OECD High Level Risk Forum research as well as the country discussions that were held during OECD expert meetings. The chapters feature and analyse good practice examples that can be found in some countries in terms of gathering and using information for the policy making process.

Chapter 4 presents a concluding discussion and an outlook for possible research in future.

Notes

[1] In the second semester of 2016 data were collected for 34/39 Adherents to the Recommendation on the Governance of Critical Risks (Only the Czech Republic, Belgium, Hungary, Morocco and Tunisia did not respond).

[2] **Damage** or **direct economic loss** is the monetary replacement value of physical assets wholly or partly destroyed, built to the same standards that prevailed prior to the disaster (GFDRR, 2017; UNISDR, 2016).

[3] **Losses** or **indirect economic loss** are the foregone economic flows/ decline in economic value added resulting from the temporary absence of the damaged assets and/or due to any other disruption of economic activity caused by the disaster (GFDRR, 2017; UNISDR, 2016).

[4] www.preventionweb.net/drr-framework/open-ended-working-group/indicators/

[5] The online OECD survey was filled out by 17 countries (Australia, Austria, Canada, Colombia, Costa Rica, Denmark, Estonia, Finland, France, Japan, Israel, Mexico, Norway, Poland, Slovak Republic, Sweden, and Turkey). Annex B provides the survey and the full list of names of the responding institution in each country.

1. Improving the Evidence Base on the Costs of Disasters

OECD countries are exposed to a range of hazards that cause disruptions to socio-economic activities and lives. Despite this, decision-makers currently rely on an incomplete record of the damages and losses caused by past disaster events. Often, the picture of evidence on disaster risk management expenditure is no more complete. This chapter illustrates that there is value in knowing the real cost of disasters. On a macro level, data on the socio-economic impact of disasters as well as the public expenditures invested to reducing them enables an evaluation of countries' strategies and disaster risk management policies overall. On a project level, such data is useful to improve the effectiveness of resource allocation decisions. Overall, this information is valuable to make the case for investments in disaster risk management by all of society's actors.

1.1. The rationale for improving the evidence base on the costs of disasters

Policy makers often rely on scattered and incomplete data on the socio-economic impact of disasters. The OECD survey shows that only half of responding OECD and partner countries (in total 17) have a national repository for disaster damage and losses data in place. In many countries disaster damage and loss data are collected separately by different line ministries responsible for the management of specific types of hazard, and hence they only collect information about the type of risks they manage. In countries where national repositories have been established, they are often quite comprehensive and offer good practice insights, such as in Canada (Box 1.1).

Box 1.1. The Canadian Disaster Database: A good country practice in recording natural disaster losses and damages

The Canadian Disaster Database (CDD), managed by Public Safety Canada, is a comprehensive and publicly and web accessible multi-hazard repository of historical information on disaster events and their impacts, recording its earliest events in 1900. The majority of events included in the database occurred in Canada, but records of disasters that happened abroad, but directly affected Canadians, are also kept. To be featured in the database, an event has to meet at least one of the following thresholds:

- 10 or more people killed;
- 100 or more people affected/injured/infected/evacuated or homeless;
- An appeal for national/international assistance;
- Historical significance;
- Significant damage/interruption of normal processes such that the community affected cannot recover on its own.

As of 2017, over 1,000 events have been recorded, They are categorised by natural disasters (e.g. biological, hydro-meteorological or geological disasters), conflict-related disasters (e.g. hijacking and terrorist activities) and technological incidents (infrastructure failure, transportation accidents and explosions). In a geospatial version of the database, disaster events can be charted across a map of Canada, enabling a location-based search of events. This makes the database both a useful tool for risk communication purposes, and for hazard mapping and risk assessment purposes, such as Canada's All-Hazards Risk Assessment.

Where available, the entries include a rough estimate of the economic costs that (nominal or real values), using the Consumer Price Index (CPI) for 2010. The data is collected from authoritative sources (e.g. government reports and peer reviewed research) and is further vetted by subject matter experts on an ad hoc basis. Although not all disaster events include damage information, the high level of disaggregation enables a good overview over the past economic impacts of the hazards Canada faces. Between 1980 and 2016, for example, the brunt of economic damage was caused by meteorological-hydrological disasters, in particular floods and storms (see Figure 1.1).

Box 1.1. The Canadian Disaster Database: A good country practice in recording natural disaster losses and damages (*continued*)

Figure 1.1. Estimated total annual damage by hazard, 1980-2016

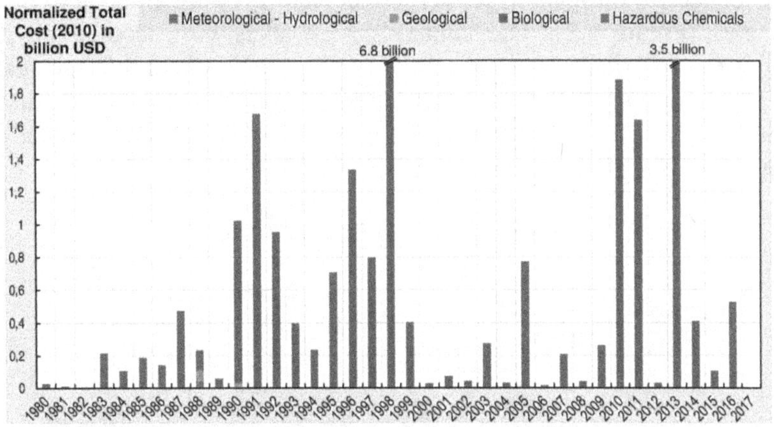

Source: Data submitted to authors by Public Safety Canada; Public Safety Canada (2017)

In addition to damage data, the database includes information regarding the number of deaths, injured and evacuated, as well as information on central government financial assistance to provincial and territorial governments provided via the Disaster Financial Assistance Arrangements (DFAA). Where applicable, information on costs incurred to other government departments and regarding payments by sub-national governments is also collected. In addition to public post-disaster payments, information on insurance payments is tracked in the database. This makes the CDD a valuable tool for monitoring central and sub-national response to disasters. This in turn contributes to the government's capacity to manage emergencies and facilitates research activities that support a unified emergency management system.

Source: 2016 OECD survey; Data submitted to authors by Public Safety Canada; Public Safety Canada (2017); Public Safety Canada (2016), Presentation at the Joint Expert Meeting on Disaster Loss Data held at the OECD in October 2016

The information collected on the economic impacts of disasters, however, is often not comparable from one disaster event to another, and even less so across countries. In some countries the "estimated economic costs" of a disaster is a category that is not clearly defined and that, depending on the size of a disaster event, may or may not contain a comprehensive assessment of direct and indirect costs. In Japan for example, a methodology is used to collect information about economic costs for a specific disaster type, namely water-related disasters (Box 1.2). The methodology distinguishes damage to assets from losses due to business interruption, and produces monetary estimates for each.

Box 1.2. The Japan survey for collecting cost information on water-related disasters

Japan's Ministry of Land, Infrastructure, Transport and Tourism (MLIT) is in charge of methods and instructions for disaster loss data collection. Disaster loss data are collected through a survey conducted by municipal and prefectural governments (Figure 1.2). The annual survey takes into account all damages occurred between January 1st and December 31st and covers damages caused by floods, landside inundation, storm surges, tsunamis, sediment discharges, landslides and steep slope failures. The survey covers all water-related disaster damages regardless of their scale.

Figure 1.2. Data collection process

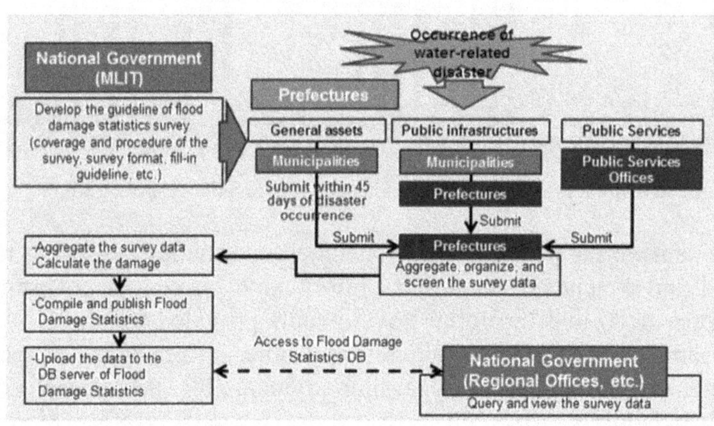

Source: MLIT (2016)

The statistics on flood damages consist of the following three components:

1) **Damages to general properties**: houses, residential properties, assets owned by fishermen/farmers, business assets, agricultural products. The municipal governments are responsible to collect data regarding damages to general properties. When transformed to monetary damage, general property damage information is separated into eight different types of general properties:

- Monetary damages to houses
- Monetary damages to household properties
- Monetary damages to business assets
- Monetary damages to assets owned by fishermen and farmers
- Monetary losses due to business interruption (Indirect loss)
- Emergency cost of households
- Emergency cost of businesses
- Monetary damages to agricultural products

2) **Damages to public works facilities**: flood control facilities for rivers, flood control facilities in coasts, facilities for landslide control, facilities to control steep slope failure, roads, bridges, ports and harbours, sewage system, parks, and other facilities in urban areas. The municipal and prefectural governments are responsible for collecting damages to public works facilities.

Box 1.2. Japan survey for water-related disasters (*continued*)

3) **Damages to public services and utilities**: railway/streetcar companies, operators of regular road passenger transport, operators of regular road freight transport, telecommunication companies, electric power companies, gas companies, water companies. The prefectural governments are responsible for collecting damages to public services and utilities.

The damages to general properties and the damages to the public works facilities are direct loss, while damage assessments for public services and utilities include both direct and indirect loss. In principle, the calculation of damages is made as follows:

Magnitude of flood damages* x Unit Value** x Depth of flood water

* Total area, the number of buildings and employees, etc.

** Unit Value for each damage category is determined via the national government survey.

Source: MLIT (2016), Presentation at the Joint Expert Meeting on Disaster Loss Data held at the OECD in October 2016

One approach to establishing disaster damage and loss information systematically is to record physical damages as a first step, and transform these damage estimates into monetary values as a second step. This is also helpful for the purpose of comparability across countries. To measure the achievement of one of the seven core objectives of the Sendai Framework to "Reduce the direct losses from disasters in relation to global gross domestic product", the Open-ended Intergovernmental Expert Working Group (OEIWG) agreed to take such an iterative approach to measuring disaster damages (Box 1.3). The approach decomposes "direct losses", i.e. damages, in five different direct loss categories, and then aggregates the direct economic losses within each of them. For example, direct agricultural loss is aggregated in terms of losses to crops, livestock, fisheries, or forests and associated infrastructures. For damages to housing, the indicator distinguishes the collection of data on the number of damaged or destroyed dwellings. Direct economic loss is then calculated in monetary terms based on a method chosen by each individual country.

Box 1.3. Sendai Framework indicators on measuring direct economic losses from disasters

The Open-ended Intergovernmental Expert Working Group (OEIWG) for establishing indicators to measure progress in implementing the seven global targets of the Sendai Framework took an iterative approach to measuring direct losses from disasters, which pertains to one of the seven targets, namely the reduction of direct economic losses attributed to disasters in relation to global domestic product. The agreed upon approach requires countries to report physical damage information across five selected economic sectors (agriculture, productive assets, housing, critical infrastructure and cultural heritage).

C-1 (compound) Direct economic loss attributed to disasters in relation to global gross domestic product.

C-2 Direct agricultural loss attributed to disasters. Agriculture is understood to include the crops, livestock, fisheries, apiculture, aquaculture and forest sectors as well as associated facilities and infrastructure.

C-3 Direct economic loss to all other damaged or destroyed productive assets attributed to disasters. Productive assets would be disaggregated by economic sector, including services, according to standard international classifications. Countries would report against those economic sectors relevant to their economies. This would be described in the associated metadata.

C-4 Direct economic loss in the housing sector attributed to disasters. Data would be disaggregated according to damaged and destroyed dwellings.

C-5 Direct economic loss resulting from damaged or destroyed critical infrastructure attributed to disasters. The decision regarding those elements of critical infrastructure to be included in the calculation will be left to the Member States and described in the accompanying metadata. Protective infrastructure and green infrastructure should be included where relevant.

C-6 Direct economic loss to cultural heritage damaged or destroyed attributed to disasters.

Source: UN General Assembly (2016). Report of the open-ended intergovernmental expert working group on indicators and terminology relating to disaster risk reduction. http://www.preventionweb.net/drr-framework/open-ended-working-group/

The survey shows that some countries collect data on the socio-economic impact of disasters, but transforming this data to match the adopted indicators remains a work in progress. In some countries, such as Sweden (Box 1.4), the majority of disaster data for the last decade (2005-2015) has already been transformed in line with the adopted indicators.

Box 1.4. Making Swedish disaster loss data compatible with the Sendai Framework indicators

In recognition of the requirements of the adopted indicators to measure progress in achieving the seven global targets put forward by the Sendai Framework, the Swedish Civil Contingencies Agency as the Swedish lead institution for the governance of critical risks has launched a process to transform available disaster impact data in line with the agreed indicators. As a first step, data regarding disasters that have occurred within Sweden's borders in the decade between 2005 and 2015 has been assessed towards their compatibility with the Sendai Framework (Figure 1.3).

Figure 1.3. Compatibility of Swedish disaster impact data with the Sendai Framework indicators

Global Target A			Global Target B			Global Target C			Global Target D		
Indicator	Compatibility		Indicator	Compatibility		Indicator	Compatibility		Indicator	Compatibility	
	Yes	No		Yes	No		Yes	No		Yes	No
A-1 (compound) deaths & missing persons due to disasters/ 100,000	X		B-1 (compound) directly affected people /100,000	X		C-1 (compound) Direct economic loss due to disasters in relation to global GDP	X		D-1 (compound) Damage to critical infrastructure due to disasters	X	
A-2 deaths due to disasters/ 100,000	X		B-2 injured/ ill due to disasters/100,000	X		C-2 Direct agricultural loss due to disasters	X		D-2 Destroyed/ damaged health facilities due to disasters.	X	
A-3 missing persons due to disasters/ 100,000	X		B-3 people with dwellings damaged by disaster	X		C-3 Direct economic loss to all other damaged/ destroyed productive assets due to disasters.	X		D-3 Destroyed/ damaged educational facilities due to disasters.	X	
			B-4 people with dwellings destroyed by disaster	X		C-4 Direct economic loss in housing sector due to disasters.	X		D-4 Other destroyed/ damaged critical infrastructure units & facilities due to disasters.	X	
			B-5 people with livelihoods disrupted or destroyed by disaster		X	C-5 Direct economic loss due to damaged/ destroyed critical infrastructure due to disasters	X		D-5 (compound) Disruptions to basic services due to disasters.		X
						C-6 Direct economic loss to cultural heritage damaged/ destroyed due to disasters	X		D-6 Number of disruptions to educational services attributed to disasters.		X
									D-7 Number of disruptions to health services attributed to disasters		X
									D-8 Number of disruptions to other basic services attributed to disasters		X

Source: 2016 OECD survey; Data submitted to authors by Swedish Civil Contingencies Agency

Box 1.5. Making Swedish disaster loss data compatible with the Sendai Framework indicators

Although the majority of data for this period has been transformed to correspond to the global indicators, not all indicators fully correspond to the final indicators yet. In the Swedish dataset, indicator B3, for example, is disaggregated into B3a (number of evacuated people) and B3b (No of relocated people). In some cases, the Swedish Sendai Framework dataset has been expanded with additional indicators, such as an indicator on exposed people added under B and an indicator on damaged tourist infrastructure facilities under D. Data on indicators B5 and D5-8 has not been adjusted yet. In addition to the remaining gaps in terms of data transformation, there are gaps in the data available for the individual disasters.

Source: 2016 OECD survey; Data submitted to authors by Swedish Civil Contingencies Agency; UNISDR (2016)

The importance of assessing critical infrastructure damage and losses

For OECD countries two specific areas of economic cost accounting from disasters are important. The first is the systematic assessment of damage to critical infrastructure. The second is the measurement of indirect or business interruption losses.

Critical infrastructure failure has repeatedly been a cause of triggering cascade effects of major disasters. Disruptions to critical infrastructure systems, such as energy, transport, water supply and sanitation and telecommunications, can act as vectors to spread the negative impacts of disasters. For example, Hurricane Sandy struck New Jersey and New York in fall 2012, leaving in its wake roughly USD 68 billion in damages and major impacts on the energy, transportation, communications, water, and health sectors in the greater New York-New Jersey metropolitan area (Flynn, 2015). An estimated 8.5 million households suffered from electricity shortages and 5.4 million people were affected by the loss of subway services. The damages to transport services alone were estimated at more than USD 10 billion (OECD, 2014). Following landfall, unanticipated interdependencies of the highly networked fuel supply and distribution system and the electric power sector along the East Coast of the United States became evident (NACS, 2013).

Damage to critical systems can lead to large economic knock-on impacts by disrupting business for longer periods than the actual disaster event. These functions are fundamental to the overall wellbeing of the populations affected by a disaster, and can either bolster, or hinder, their ability to recover. This underlines the importance for OECD countries to systematically document critical infrastructure failures and damage to assets. On the one hand such assessments are an important financial planning tool, especially for those assets that a government is ultimately financially liable for in case of a disaster. On the other hand, a solid evidence base on damage to critical infrastructure and their knock-on effects allows governments to understand their vulnerabilities in critical infrastructure systems better and improve disaster risk reduction efforts to avoid negative economic impacts in the future.

The Sendai Framework indicators included infrastructure damage in the direct loss Target C, but did not agree on concrete information on physical damage that shall be reported by countries and left it to countries to include what is appropriate for them in terms of critical infrastructure (Box 1.3). In Target D, which is specifically dedicated to reducing damage to critical infrastructure, the Sendai Framework focuses on damage and disruptions to health and education facilities and suggests that countries report on additional numbers of critical infrastructure facilities damaged or disrupted that they may wish to report upon. For OECD countries the focus on health and educational facilities is not sufficiently far-reaching when the aim is to manage critical infrastructure damage and its potential knock-on economic impacts. A large number of OECD countries have embraced a more comprehensive take on critical infrastructure, focusing on sectors and facilities that provide services essential to a country's socio-economic functioning. This includes the energy sector, transportation infrastructure, communication and information communication technology, as well as basic services, such as health and financial services and food and water provision (Figure 1.4).

Figure 1.4. Critical infrastructure sectors identified in OECD countries

Sector	Number of countries
Transport networks/nodes	30
Electricity/gas/fuel distribution networks	29
Electricity/gas/fuel production sites	29
Telecommunications networks	28
Protective assets (e.g. flood barriers and.	25
Data centres	24
Fibre optic interconnectors	23
Telecommunication satellites	19
Health care and public health sector	7
Systems of industrial production	6
Financial service institutions	5
Nuclear power plants and chemical waste.	5
Government facilities	4
Water and wastewater systems	4
Food supply	4
Defense and social security	3
Metereological and space service	3
Emergency services	3
Research centres	2
Postal services	1

0 5 10 15 20 25 30 35

Number of countries

Source: OECD, *forthcoming*

Losses arise from disaster related business interruption and the associated disruption in the flow of goods and services – both in areas directly affected by the hazard and in areas that have not directly been affected. Business interruption losses include the temporary or permanent loss of employment due to workplace destruction or obstruction to travel to work or a lack or destruction of an input necessary to continue work. Indirect losses also include losses in terms of forgone consumption or price increases due to increased scarcity faced by consumers. Indirect losses can be significant and particularly important to some stakeholder groups, such as small and medium enterprises that do not have business interruption insurance or need to rely on the government for compensation. In the Sendai Framework this loss dimension has been acknowledged in the definitions' part of the agreement, but is not included as a formal target or indicator.

Owing to the interconnectedness of economies, spill-over effects are not limited to one country. This creates an interest in proper and reliable damage data even in economies with relatively low direct exposure to extreme hazards. Private businesses in particular have a genuine interest in learning about disaster impacts in other economies. For instance, in Hong Kong, China, where the manufacturing industry has key supply linkages with companies in Japan, the government conveyed to the Japanese Government a request for more information on the post-disaster situation in Japan following the Great East Japan Earthquake. The official information on damages to business and connected supply interruptions was then shared with the respective partner industries in Hong Kong (OECD, 2015).

Although indirect losses are a particularly important dimension for informing effective risk management strategies in OECD countries, including decisions on risk transfer strategies, most of the countries the OECD surveyed reported on damages, or direct losses, only. In some countries, such as Finland, an estimation of the losses, or indirect damage, is conducted, but only for major disaster events, as the country-wide impacts of smaller disasters tend to be low enough for many OECD economies to absorb them, Although the definition of "economic costs" has different and even ambiguous meanings, there are some good practices in countries where a clear definition is provided on how economic costs are calculated. In the case of water-related disasters in Japan, for example, the economic cost definition makes a clear distinction between indirect business interruption losses and direct losses (Box 1.2). Few standards suggest how to calculate this category of losses. One such method has been proposed by the UN Economic Commission for Latin America and the Caribbean (ECLAC) (see Box 1.6).

Box 1.6. Calculating indirect losses – the UN ECLAC approach

One methodology calculating indirect losses caused by disasters has been developed by the UN Economic Commission for Latin America and the Caribbean (ECLAC). The ECLAC methodology estimates the damages (direct costs) and losses (indirect costs) of disasters on the overall economy of the affected country, as well as on the household level (Figure 1.5). It includes:

- The replacement value of totally or partially destroyed physical assets;
- Losses in the flow of the economy arising from the temporary absence of the damaged assets;
- The resulting impact on post-disaster economic performance (economic growth, government fiscal's position and the balance of payments).

Figure 1.5. Conceptual framework

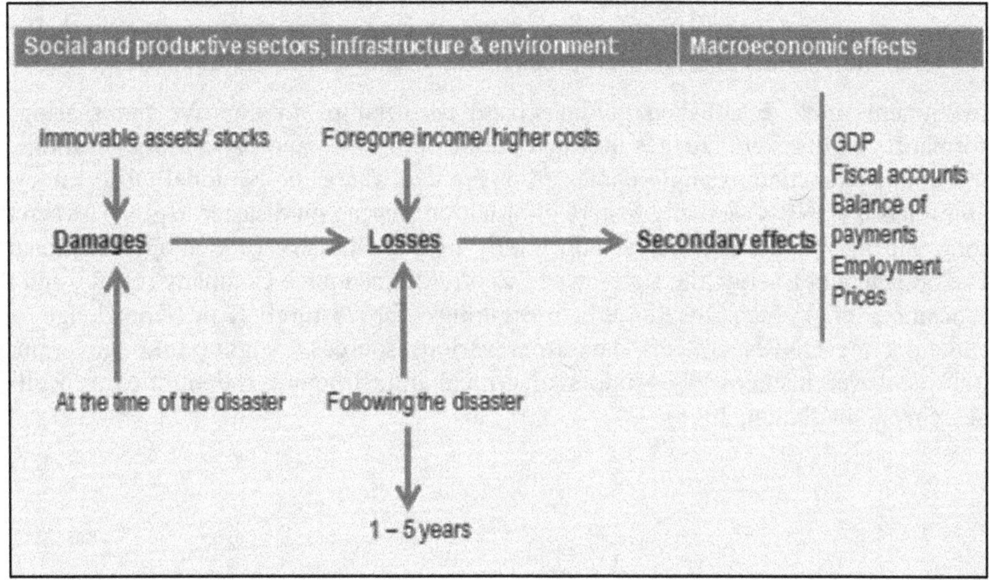

Source: based on ECLAC (2016)

Source: UN ECLAC (2016). Handbook for Disaster Assessment. United Nations Commission for Latin America and the Caribbean, ttp://repositorio.cepal.org/bitstream/handle/11362/36823/S2013817_en.pdf?sequence=1&isAllowed=y

The value of disaster loss data collected by non-government agencies

Governments are not the only sources of disaster loss information within or across countries. Other stakeholders, such as private (or public) insurance and reinsurance organisations or insurance associations, have collected such information for a long time on national and international level. In Australia, for example, the Insurance Council of Australia has a catastrophe claims dataset to track disaster related insured losses of more than AUD 10 million, while in the Czech Republic the National Bank collects data from insurance companies on the number and volume of claims related to property (OECD, 2015).

Data on insured losses are often more comprehensive, systematically recorded and depict valuable trends in disaster losses over time. They can also provide a basis for estimating overall economic losses (Box 1.7). In Switzerland, for instance, private insurance companies record insured damages and losses from natural catastrophes in a non-public repository for supervisory purposes. As insurance deductibles are standardised in Switzerland, this data can be used to reconstruct non-insured losses without risking trend distortions (OECD, 2015). Such a trend analysis is useful to uncover resilience gaps (i.e. instances of high or repeat losses), which may require a policy response, e.g. in the form of targeted investments in disaster risk reduction (Neumeyer and Barthel, 2011).

Governments have established public-private partnerships to improve the sharing of information on disaster damages between public authorities and private organisations. A good country practice example comes from France, where the National Observatory of Natural Risks (ONRN) actively fosters information sharing on disaster losses between the public and the private sectors. Set up jointly by the Ministry of Ecology, Sustainable Development and Energy, the state-owned Central Reinsurance Company (CCR), and the Association of French Insurance Undertakings for Natural Risk Knowledge and Reduction, the ONRN collects data from various sources, ranging from government authorities over insurers to operators of critical infrastructure and utilities as well as researchers (Nussbaum, 2016).

Box 1.7. Insured loss information as a basis for analysing disaster trends and estimating associated economic losses

The insurance industry has collected information on insured disaster losses for a long time and can provide comprehensive insights into trends in losses over time. For example, Swiss Re's sigma catastrophe database is an international commercial database that records both natural and man-made disasters and their associated insured losses on a global scale. It has recorded over 10,000 events since 1970 and provides geocoded, national level information on insured losses. With NatCatService Munich Re operates a similar database that features data since 1980.

Figure 1.6. Global disaster losses 1970-2014

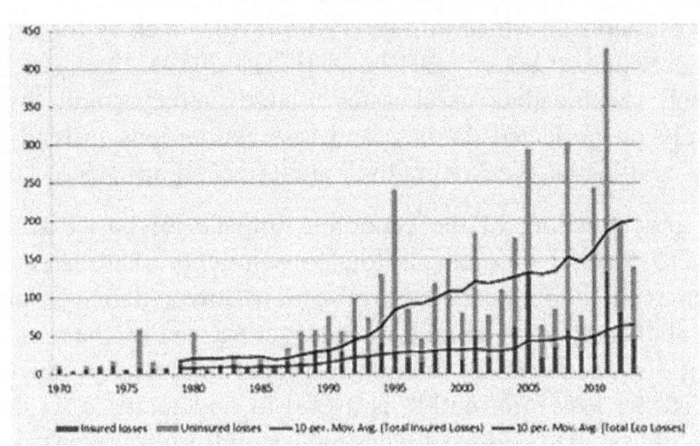

Source: Swiss Re (2014)

Figure 1.7. Using insured loss information to estimate economic loss

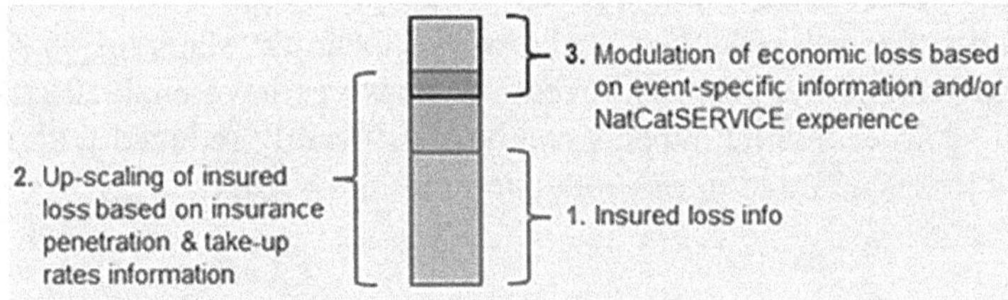

Source: Munich Re, NatCatSERVICE (2016)

Although the data collected by the insurance industry typically focuses on insured losses only, they allow for analysing valuable disaster cost trends over time and can build the basis for estimations of overall economic losses, especially if used in connection with information on insurance penetration and take-up rates (Figures 1.6 and 1.7).

Source: Munich Re (2016), Presentation at the Joint Expert Meeting on Disaster Loss Data held at the OECD in October 2016; Swiss Re (2014). Presentation at the "Improving the Measurement on the Costs of Disasters Meeting" held at the OECD in November 2014

Economic cost information for project level decisions and macro policy evaluations

The effectiveness of disaster risk reduction measures depends strongly on the capacity to identify disaster risks and to understand their potential impacts. Public policy decisions need to be informed by the trade-offs and benefits of different investment options, including what can be considered an acceptable level of risk under the relevant circumstances. Decision-support tools for individual disaster risk reduction projects, such as cost-benefit or cost-effectiveness analyses (CBA), can help governments identify the marginal cost of achieving desired levels of preparedness, prevention or mitigation measures in light of competing demands for resource allocations. Such tools provide public authorities with a method to systematically compare the advantages and disadvantages of planned investments. They also enable an identification of risks valued against their probability of occurrence and potential damage, based on which the avoidance cost can be calculated. In a number of OECD countries the use of such tools is obligatory for investments above certain threshold levels, such as for example in Austria, France and Switzerland (OECD, 2017a; OECD, 2014). Yet, in the absence of comprehensive and reliable data on disaster related damages and losses, cost benefit analysis has to rely on projected damage and loss estimations instead of observed past recorded damages and losses, weakening their analytical significance.

Without a clear understanding of the economic impacts of past disasters it is hard to evaluate at a macro level if a country's total investments in disaster risk management have actually achieved their intended purpose – to lower damages and losses due to disasters. On a global level, such an ambitious target was set by the Sendai Framework in terms of reducing disaster losses in relation to global domestic product. Systematic and comprehensive disaster loss information is useful to understand how much a country is saving in terms of avoided losses given the overall investments in risk reduction measures. A lack of standard methods to measure the economic cost of disasters on the other hand compromises the comparability of data over time, making an assessment of achievements and shortcomings difficult (Guha-Sapir et al., 2013). In countries, where such information is collected, this proved to be an effective argument in favour of investments in disaster risk reduction. In Japan, for example, statistics on socio-economic damages and losses and the cost of prevention measures have enabled risk managers to show that total socio-economic impacts can be significantly reduced with only a fraction of the expected losses invested in risk reduction measures (Box 1.8).

Box 1.8. Using disaster damage and loss data to measure the effectiveness of risk reduction investments in Japan

Information on socio-economic damages and losses are key factors necessary to evaluate the effectiveness of resilience measures. In Japan, policy makers have recognized and embraced the potential of such evaluations. Using the data on actual damage, such as caused by the 2000 Tokai Storm in central Japan, in combination with the cost information on implemented preventive measures as decided after the storm, enabled risk managers with the necessary information to calculate the effectiveness of the investments in flood risk management measures taken by central and local governments (Figure 1.8).

Figure 1.8. Using disaster loss data simulations to assess effectiveness (2000 Tokai Storm)

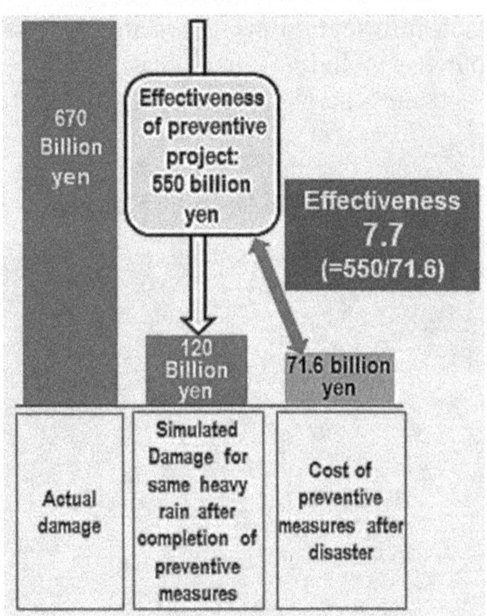

Source: MLIT (2016)

Source: MLIT (2016), Presentation at the Joint Expert Meeting on Disaster Loss Data held at the OECD in October 2016

Comprehensive damage and loss data foster a whole-of-society engagement in disaster risk management

Comprehensive data on the costs of disasters is not only important to inform public policy decisions, but is vital in a wider debate that fosters a whole-of-society engagement in disaster risk management. In some countries disaster damage and loss data are already used strategically to boost citizens' and businesses' disaster risk awareness. In Australia, for example, information on insured losses is integrated in an innovative risk communication tool that allows a mapping of past disasters and their socio-economic impacts throughout Australia (Box 1.9).

Box 1.9. Australia's Disaster Resilience Knowledge Hub: the use of disaster data for risk communication

The Australian Disaster Resilience Knowledge Hub (the 'Knowledge Hub') houses historical information about disasters that have affected Australia, as well as valuable resources and relevant research to inform policy development, decision making and good practice in disaster resilience. The Knowledge Hub supports implementation of the National Strategy for Disaster Resilience by promoting knowledge sharing and the principle of shared responsibility.

The Disaster Mapper supports engagement with the Australian disasters collection, aiding users to understand historical disasters in a broader context. Filtering the map results by hazard type (Figure 1.9) allows users to understand the types of hazards that have affected different parts of the country. Clicking on an individual disaster icon provides further socio-economic information to contextualise the impact. Information presented in the Disaster Mapper is drawn from a range of sources including insurance figures, reporting from lead emergency services agencies across the states and territories and academic sources.

Figure 1.9. Australian Disaster Mapper

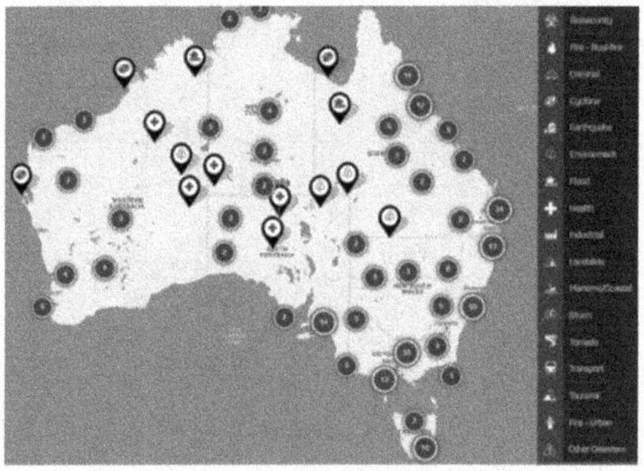

Source: Australian Institute for Disaster Resilience, 2017

Source: Australian Institute for Disaster Resilience 2017, https://knowledge.aidr.org.au/

1.2. The benefits of recording public disaster risk management expenditures

Policy makers in many OECD countries have had to rely on an incomplete picture of their country's spending on disaster risk management. The OECD survey showed that data on expenditure on disaster risk management measures is collected in less than half of the responding countries. Where data is collected, it usually focuses on specific spending categories. Australia, for example, collects this information regularly, but does so only for rehabilitation investments and not for overall risk management. In France, this has been done only for prevention investments. In addition, disaster risk management expenditure tracking in most countries focuses on the central government level, and often do not reflect the expenditures made at sub-national levels. In countries where data is collected on sub-national expenditures, it is often done separately from the tracking of central spending. In Japan, central government budget data for both ex-ante and ex-post disaster management expenditure is annually published in the "Disaster Management in Japan, White Paper", while data on sub-national post-disaster relief and recovery expenditure is collected in a separate process and not featured in the annual White Paper (Box 1.10). In Colombia, on the other hand, disaster risk management expenditure statistics reflect central and sub-national contributions (Box 1.11).

Box 1.10. Japan's White Paper on Disaster Management

Since 1963, the Japanese Cabinet Office in cooperation with line ministries publishes an annual White Paper on Disaster Management. The White Paper provides a comprehensive overview of all aspects and current activities in disaster risk reduction and is reported annually to the ordinary session of the Diet. It outlines the status of disaster management policies and their implementation. Often, the White Paper also covers a topic of special concern to disaster management such as the challenges relating to an aging society.

As one of the elements covered in the White Paper, disaster management budgets since 1962 are listed. The budgets are broken down into four categories: Disaster Prevention, Science & Technology Research, Land Conservation and Disaster Reconstruction. Figure 1.10 illustrates the development of central government disaster risk management spending in Japan between 1980 and 2016, as tracked in the 2016 White Paper.

As one of the elements covered in the White Paper, disaster management budgets since 1962 are listed. The budgets are broken down into four categories: Disaster Prevention, Science & Technology Research, Land Conservation and Disaster Reconstruction. Figure 1.11 illustrates the development of central government disaster risk management spending in Japan between 1980 and 2016, as tracked in the 2016 White Paper.

Figure 1.10. Disaster prevention and reconstruction expenditure in Japan, 1980-2016

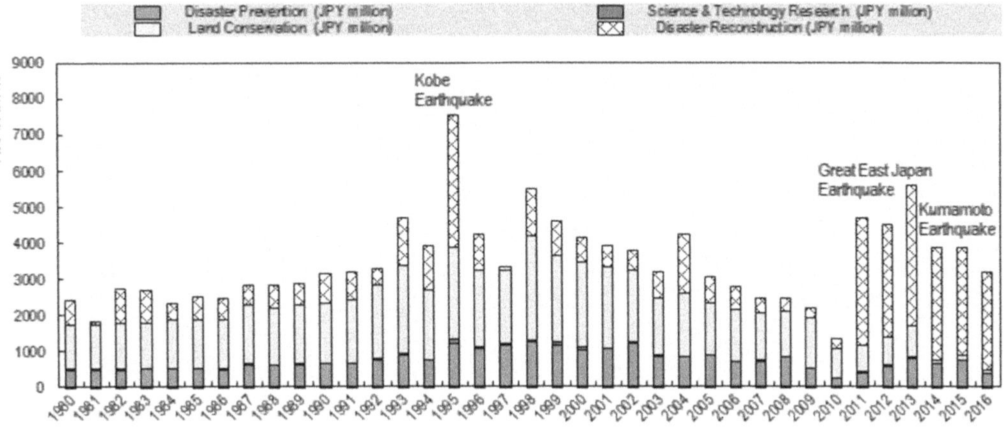

Note: In 2004 expenditure recording methods changed slightly making the comparison between budget estimates prior and after these changes less imprecise. The figures for the 2016 fiscal year are preliminary figures reflecting the initial budget.

Source: Authors, based on Cabinet Office Japan (2017)

Box 1.10. Japan's White Paper on Disaster Management (*continued*)

In addition, the White Paper also provides information regarding facility-related damages in public works, agriculture, education, public welfare, etc. (Figure 1.11), using data from various ministries and agencies. The White Paper also features more general hazard information, such as hazard maps, and occurrence of hazardous events in Japan and elsewhere.

Figure 1.11. Trends in Facility-Related Damage, Actual and as a Percentage of GDP

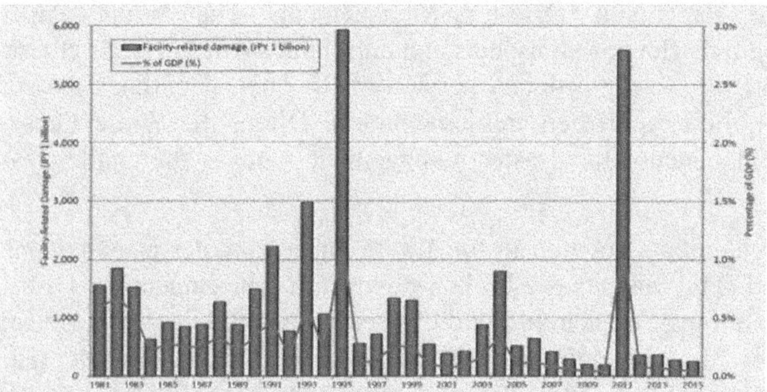

Source: Cabinet Office Japan (2017)

Source: Cabinet Office Japan (2017). White Paper Disaster Management in Japan 2017, www.bousai.go.jp/kyoiku/panf/pdf/WP2017_DM_Full_Version.pdf

Box 1.11. Disaster risk management expenditure in Colombia

Although records are not publicly accessible, research shows that the Colombian government has tracked disaster risk management expenditure throughout levels of government in the past. The available data provides an overview over disaster risk management expenditure spent both at central and at sub-national level and illustrates priorities in disaster risk management spending. The records show that the national budget allocation for both disaster prevention and mitigation has been steadily increasing (Figure 1.12). Despite consistent investments in disaster risk prevention and mitigation measures, recovery and reconstruction spending in the aftermath of disasters has remained substantial. In fact, on average, post-disaster spending has had an average growth rate of 65.26% per year (1998-2008), while pre-disaster spending only increased by 22.08% over the same period.

Figure 1.12. Pre- and Post-disaster government spending in Colombia, 2004 – 2007

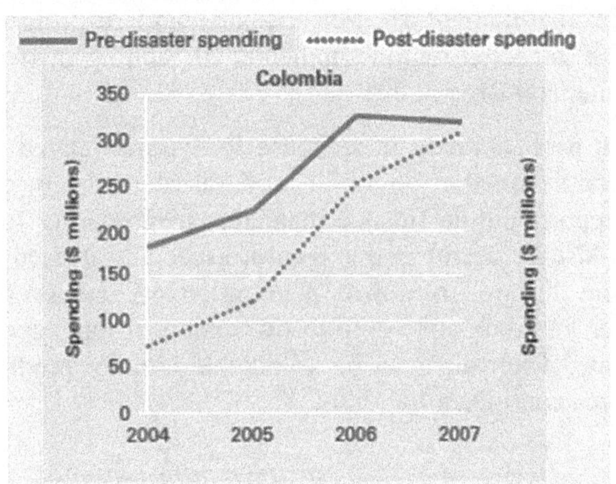

Source: De la Fuente, A. (2010)

At municipal level, the focus on ex-ante investments has been even more pronounced than at central level, with pre-disaster expenditure consistently outpacing the amount of resources devoted to relief and recovery. While recovery and reconstruction spending has been between 73 and 310 million USD per year in the 2004-07 period, pre-disaster expenditure at sub-national level has gone beyond 183 million USD in each year (De la Fuente, 2010). Between 2002 and 2008, municipalities' investment in disaster risk reduction has even exceeded disaster risk prevention and mitigation spending at central level. Although this is in part due to the concentration of disaster risk management responsibilities at municipal level, the available data shows that in the aftermath of great disasters, such as during the 2010 rainy season that saw numerous instances of flooding and landslides, the central government has increased their investments into ex-ante disaster risk management spending (World Bank and GFDRR, 2012).

Source: De la Fuente, A. (2010). Government Expenditures in Pre and Post Disaster Risk Management, Background Note for World Bank–U.N. Assessment on the Economics of Disaster Risk Reduction. Natural Hazards, Unnatural Disasters: The Economics of Effective Prevention; World Bank and Global Facility for Disaster Reduction and Recovery (GFDRR) (2012). Analysis of Disaster Risk Management in Colombia A Contribution to the Creation of Public Policies.

Tracking disaster risk management expenditure in a central framework enables a better understanding of potential disaster-related contingent liabilities

Governments frequently shoulder a large extent of the costs related to disaster recovery and compensation, particularly where insurance coverage is limited (Gamper et al., 2017). In most cases, such costs are for example due to the obligation to restore public assets and services, but they may also include implicit contingent liabilities, i.e. unanticipated expenditures that are not budgeted for but for which there is some moral expectation that they will be made. When disaster risk-related contingent liabilities materialise, major budget volatility may follow. The Great East Japan Earthquake in 2011, for example, resulted in government spending that represented an estimated 20.7% of the general account budget in the 2012 fiscal year alone, totalling around USD 36.5 billion. Much of this was financed through supplementary budgets, relying largely on the issue of bonds and loans, cuts in previously authorised expenditure and budget surplus appropriations from the surplus of the previous fiscal year (Sato and Boudreau, 2012). Hurricane Sandy in 2012, which impacted twelve states along the East Coast of the United States, plus the District of Columbia, resulted in a similar fiscal response. To finance the recovery and reconstruction in the aftermath of Hurricane Sandy and to mitigate the damage from future disasters in the impacted region supplemental funding of over USD 50.7 billion were redirected (Painter and Brown, 2013).

Reliable evidence on past spending in response to disaster-related contingent liabilities helps create awareness for the possibility of disaster-related contingent liabilities materialising and supports public finance managers in preparing for this. Data on past disaster damage can also be useful in this regard, especially if used in combination with information regarding hazard insurance penetration. A comprehensive dataset that disaggregates disaster loss data according to ownership of damaged or destroyed assets (e.g. public vs. private ownership) can be a valuable tool for predicting possible future implicit disaster-related contingent liabilities.

Transparency in the allocation of disaster risk management expenditures

The OECD survey on the governance of critical risks showed that overall the majority of responding countries rated themselves as relatively low in the fulfilment of the recommendation to demonstrate transparency and accountability in risk-related decision making. This includes their self-assessment about honest and realistic dialogue between stakeholders on the cost-effectiveness of various mitigation, response and recovery options as well as measures to validate the integrity of disaster risk management, all of which would benefit from a comprehensive and transparent synopsis of disaster risk management-related expenditure. The 2016 OECD survey also found that a majority of responding countries would welcome the development of an OECD framework on disaster risk management-related expenditure.

Much like in other policy areas risk management authorities have an obligation to allocate public resources in a transparent way. Transparent and accessible disaster risk management spending holds decision-makers accountable and contributes to sounder and more effective public spending. Although fiscal transparency is only one dimension of public accountability, it is nonetheless an important dimension that helps ensure that public investments reach their intended target and are spent effectively (OECD, 2017b).

1.3. Conclusion

This chapter illustrates the value in improving the evidence base on the cost of disasters – both in terms of measuring the socio-economic impacts of disasters and in terms of better understanding the cost of avoiding or reducing them. An understanding of how much is spent on managing the consequences of disasters helps to evaluate the longer term benefits of investments to reduce disaster damages and losses. Figures on disaster risk management expenditure provide the basis for holding decision-makers accountable and inform more effective public spending.

On a macro level, coherent data on the socio-economic impact of past disasters enables an evaluation of countries' progress in reducing disaster risk, while on a project level such data is useful to improve the effectiveness of resource allocation decisions. For OECD countries particular value lies in systematically assessing the economic impact of business interruptions and damage to critical infrastructures. Overall, this information is valuable to make the case for investments in disaster risk reduction and to boost the disaster risk awareness of both decision-makers and societal actors at large. To improve the existing evidence base on both damages and losses cooperation between government agencies and non-governmental stakeholders can hold great potential that has not been tapped in most countries.

References

Cabinet Office Japan (2017). White Paper Disaster Management in Japan 2017, www.bousai.go.jp/kyoiku/panf/pdf/WP2017_DM_Full_Version.pdf

De la Fuente, A. (2010). Government Expenditures in Pre and Post Disaster Risk Management, Background Note for World Bank–U.N. Assessment on the Economics of Disaster Risk Reduction. Natural Hazards, Unnatural Disasters: The Economics of Effective Prevention; www.gfdrr.org/sites/gfdrr/files/Country%20Disaster%20Expenditures%20Note.pdf

Flynn, S.E. (2015). Bolstering Critical Infrastructure Resilience After Superstorm Sandy: Lessons for New York and the Nation, https://hazdoc.colorado.edu/handle/10590/3003

Gamper, C., Signer, B., Alton, L. and M. Petrie (2017). Managing disaster-related contingent liabilities in public finance frameworks, OECD Publishing, Paris, http://dx.doi.org/10.1787/a6e0265a-en

Guha-Sapir, D. and I., Santos (2013). The Economic Impacts of Natural Disasters, Oxford University Press, New York

MLIT (2016). Presentation at the Joint Expert Meeting on Disaster Loss Data held at the OECD, www.slideshare.net/OECD-GOV/economic-loss-accounting-in-japan-tomoyuki-okada-mlit

Munich Re (2016). Presentation at the Joint Expert Meeting on Disaster Loss Data held at the OECD, www.slideshare.net/OECD-GOV/natcatservice-jan-eichner

NACS (2013). 2013 NACS Retail Fuels Report, www.nacsonline.com/YourBusiness/FuelsReports/GasPrices_2013/Pages/How-Hurricane-Sandy-Affected-the-Fuels-Industry.aspx

Neumeyer, E. and F. Barthel (2011). Normalizing Economic Loss from Natural Disasters: A Global Analysis, Global Environmental Change, Vol. 21, No. 1, pp. 13-24, : https://ssrn.com/abstract=1720414

Nussbaum, R. (2016). Presentation at the Joint Expert Meeting on Disaster Loss Data held at the OECD, Paris, https://www.slideshare.net/OECD-GOV/mrn-french-experience-in-econ-loss-accounting-roland-nussbaum

OECD (2014). Boosting Resilience through Innovative Risk Governance, OECD Publishing, Paris, http://dx.doi.org/10.1787/9789264209114-en

OECD (2015). Disaster Risk Financing: A global survey of practices and challenges, OECD Publishing, Paris, http://dx.doi.org/10.1787/9789264234246-en

OECD (2017a), Boosting Disaster Prevention through Innovative Risk Governance: Insights from Austria, France and Switzerland, OECD Reviews of Risk Management Policies, OECD Publishing, Paris, http://dx.doi.org/10.1787/9789264281370-en.

OECD (2017b). Recommendation on Public Integrity, OECD Publishing, Paris, http://www.oecd.org/gov/ethics/Recommendation-Public-Integrity.pdf

Painter, W. and J. Brown (2013). FY2013 Supplemental Funding for Disaster Relief, https://fas.org/sgp/crs/misc/R42869.pdf

Public Safety Canada (2016). Presentation at the Joint Expert Meeting on Disaster Loss Data held at the OECD; https://www.slideshare.net/OECD-GOV/matthew-godsoe-and-c-cody-anderson-public-safety-canada-cdd

Sato, M. and L. Boudreau (2012). The Financial and Fiscal Impacts, World Bank, Washington, DC, https://openknowledge.worldbank.org/handle/10986/16165

Swiss Re (2014). Presentation at the First Improving the Measurement on the Costs of Disasters Meeting held at the OECD in November, www.slideshare.net/OECD-GOV/workshop-evidencebasecostsofdisastersbevere

UN ECLAC (2016). Handbook for Disaster Assessment. United Nations Commission for Latin America and the Caribbean, ttp://repositorio.cepal.org/bitstream/handle/11362/36823/S2013817_en.pdf?sequence=1&isAllowed=y

UNISDR (2016). Sweden serious about Sendai, United Nations Office for Disaster Risk Reduction, www.unisdr.org/archive/52863

United Nations General Assembly (2016). Report of the open-ended intergovernmental expert working group on indicators and terminology relating to disaster risk reduction. www.preventionweb.net/drr-framework/open-ended-working-group/

World Bank and Global Facility for Disaster Reduction and Recovery (GFDRR) (2012). Analysis of Disaster Risk Management in Colombia A Contribution to the Creation of Public Policies, https://www.gfdrr.org/sites/gfdrr/files/publication/Analysis_of_Disaster_Risk_Management_in_Colombia.pdf

2. Progress in measuring and accounting for disaster damage and losses in OECD countries

Disaster damage and loss data is indispensable for informing effective disaster risk reduction strategies and risk reduction investments. This chapter presents the results of an assessment of countries' progress in collecting and using disaster damage and loss information. It provides a discussion of the disaster damage and loss data repositories that have been created on an international level. It brings together results from the OECD survey, country expert meetings as well as additional desk research. It discusses the objectives of ongoing international efforts to improve the availability of country-level disaster damage and loss data and their expected impacts on countries' activities in the future.

2.1. Introduction

Resilience against natural disasters in OECD member countries is high compared to non-OECD countries. During the past 30 years, OECD member countries have experienced significantly lower average fatality rates per disaster than lower income countries, reflecting significant progress in decreasing the exposure and vulnerability to natural disasters (Figure 2.1). However, Figure 2.2 indicates that higher income OECD countries continue to experience higher estimated economic costs compared to those countries with lower income per capita. Even if the available data is coarse and leaves room only for broad trend interpretations at this moment in time, it illustrates that policy makers need a good understanding of past disaster losses. Only once a conclusive trend in economic costs can be established will policy makers be able to interpret the data as to what extent their disaster risk investments (see Chapter 3) have been effective in reducing them.

Figure 2.1. Significant decrease in fatality rates from disasters with increasing income 1980-2013

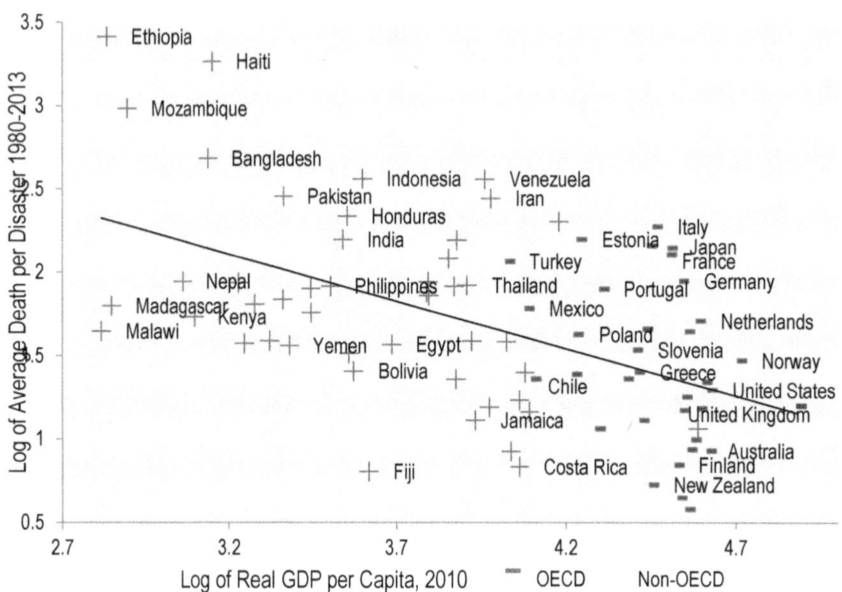

Source: OECD (2014a)

Figure 2.2. Fatality rates and economic damages to OECD countries by income quartile, 1995-2010

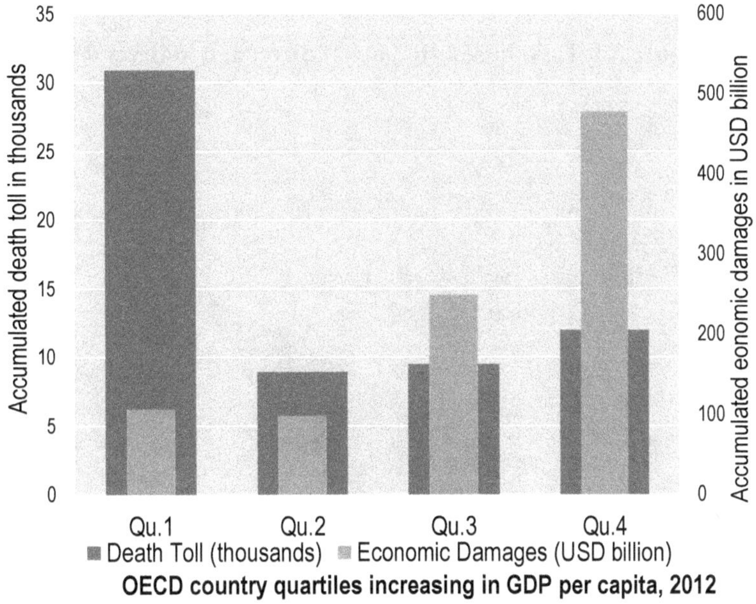

Source: OECD (2014a)

This chapter provides an overview of results of an assessment carried out by the OECD High Level Risk Forum on countries' practices and notable achievements in measuring and collecting disaster damage and loss information. As mentioned in the introduction to this report information presented here is the result of a multi-year activity of the OECD High Level Risk Forum on Assessing the Costs of Disasters. This includes information collected on disaster damages and losses through the (i) 2016 OECD survey on the "Cost of Disasters[1]; (ii) two OECD expert workshops held in 2014 and 2016[2] and (iii) complementary desk research.

The following chapter provides a brief conceptual introduction into the measurement of disaster damages and losses so as to create a basis against which country achievements are assessed. This is important as country level and international approaches on how damages and losses are measured can differ substantially. The chapter then presents a state of the art of country level data collection on ex-post disaster damages and losses. The discussion will focus on the data collection process as well as the level of quality in terms of comprehensiveness and consistency of the actual disaster damage and loss data that is collected. Before the discussion turns to the comparability of existing data across countries, some preliminary evidence on the actual use of damage and loss information for risk management policy decisions is provided. In a final discussion the chapter will present the complementary value and merit of ex-ante disaster damage and loss assessments.

2.2. Accounting for the cost of disasters: What needs to get measured and how

When accounting for the costs of disasters, different cost categories are usually distinguished as different measurement approaches are needed. While terminology can differ (Table 2.1), most often cost frameworks distinguish between direct (economic) loss (also referred to as damages) and indirect (economic) loss (also referred to as losses).

Figure 2.3 shows that total disaster losses are a combination of the direct losses that equate the replacement value of destroyed or damaged assets and the lost output that results from the absence of assets needed to maintain economic activity.

Figure 2.3. Total losses: the sum of direct and indirect losses

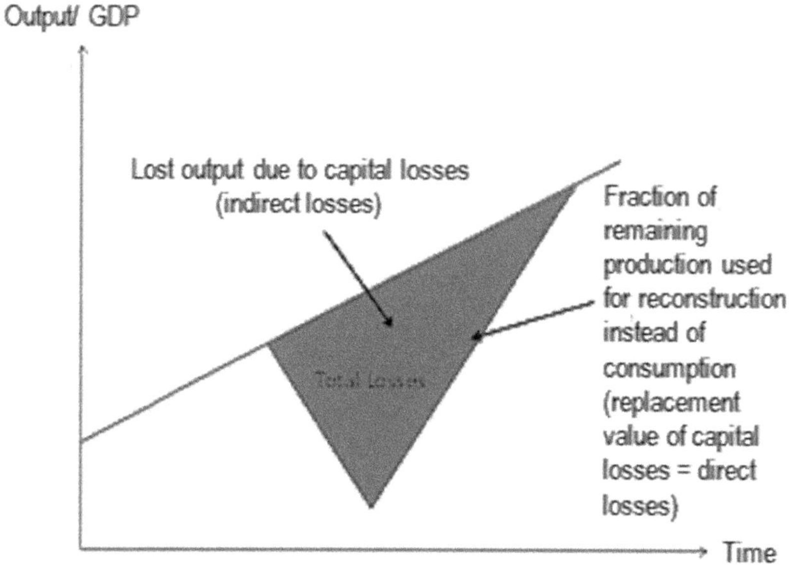

Source: Hallegatte and Przyluski, 2010

Academic literature, such as Meyer et al. (2012), often differentiate between two types of indirect economic loss to take account of the different approaches needed to measure them:

- *Direct costs* include the costs that accrue directly to assets, such as property due to the physical contact with the hazard. They include costs caused by the physical destruction of buildings, inventories, stocks, infrastructure or other assets at risk. Market prices exist for these goods and services allowing expressing relatively easily in monetary terms.
- *Losses due to business interruption* are the costs accrued by the disruption of activities in areas directly affected by the hazard. The disruption includes work that is not carried out due to workplace destruction or obstruction to travel to work or a lack or destruction of an input to continue work (e.g. electricity to run information technology systems of factory machinery). Sometimes this is referred to as primary indirect losses, because losses do not result from physical damage to property but from interruption of economic processes.
- *Indirect costs* include only those costs not caused by the hazard itself but induced by the knock-on impacts due to business interruptions caused by the disaster. This includes the failure of production by businesses due to lack of inputs by suppliers whose production was directly impacted. It also includes forgone consumption or price increases due to increased scarcity faced by customers. Indirect costs can span a longer period of time than the direct costs caused by an adverse event itself and their perseverance and degree of impact heavily depend on the system's ability to recover. Due to the complexity of assessing indirect costs, only some

rough estimates have been suggested, depending on the assessed direct losses (Hallegatte and Przyluski, 2010; Hallegatte, 2014).

The above cost categories are usually part of overall disaster loss assessments. Sometimes, in addition to the main categories distinguished above, intangible costs are added to the equation. They include costs in goods and services that are not available to buy on traditional markets and hence have no obvious price attached to them. They are referred to as non-market values or costs. Such items include for example environmental impacts, health impacts and impacts on cultural heritage. As it requires effort to express them in monetary terms, they are often left out of the calculation, leading to incomplete estimates of total costs.

To achieve a fully comprehensive understanding of disaster costs however, the costs of reconstruction and recovery and costs of planning and implementation of disaster risk management measures should be taken into account. This aspect is hardly included in existing loss assessment information captured in existing databases. The Canadian Disaster Database, for instance, is one of the few databases that tracks disaster reconstruction and recovery costs due to a specific event, albeit only as paid out by the Disaster Financial Assistance Arrangements (Public Safety Canada).

In the remainder of this report we will refer to disaster damages and losses, following the definition suggested by GFDRR (Table 2.1), as a way to distinguish direct cost and indirect cost categories. Damage thereby refers to the replacement value of physical assets wholly or partly destroyed during a disaster and losses summarise the monetary consequence in the flows of the economy that were inflicted by the temporary absence of the damaged assets (GFDRR, 2017).

Table 2.1. Terminology used to describe disaster damages and losses

	Direct loss – (disaster) damage	Indirect loss – (disaster) losses
United Nations Office for Disaster Risk Reduction/ Open-ended intergovernmental expert working group on indicators and terminology relating to disaster risk reduction	**Direct economic loss**: the monetary value of the total or partial destruction of physical assets; tends to be almost equivalent to physical damage. These are tangible and relatively easy to measure.	**Indirect economic loss**: decline in economic value added that result from direct economic loss and the human or environmental impacts of a disaster. They can occur inside or outside of the hazard area and often have a time lag. As a result they may be intangible or difficult to measure.
Global Facility for Disaster Risk Reduction - World Bank	**Damage**: the replacement value of physical assets fully or in part destroyed by a hazardous event	**Losses**: the monetary consequence in the flows of the economy that were inflicted by the temporary absence of the damaged assets
United Nations Economic Commission for Latin America and the Caribbean	**Damage**: effects the disaster has on the assets of each sector, expressed in monetary terms.	**Losses and additional costs** are disruptions to flows resulting from a disaster. Because they have different financial implications, it is necessary to differentiate: a) **Losses**: goods that go unproduced and services that go un-provided during a period running from the time the disaster occurs until full recovery and reconstruction is achieved. (b) **Additional costs**: outlays required to produce goods and provide services due to a disaster.
Joint Research Centre (European Union)	**Disaster damage**: destruction of physical assets that measured in physical units and can be expressed in monetary terms, using replacement costs at pre-disaster value as a proxy.	**Disaster loss**: market-based adverse economic impact; can be direct or indirect.
	Direct loss: monetary value of physical damage to capital assets that roughly equates stock losses	**Indirect loss**: damage to the flow of goods and services; may include reduced levels of productivity and loss of revenue caused by damage to supporting infrastructure or due to increases in the price of inputs
Other definitions	**Direct tangible costs**: costs that accrue directly to assets due to the physical contact with the hazard; 'tangible' implies that a market and prices exist for these goods and services	**Indirect costs**: only those costs not caused by the hazard itself but induced by the knock-on impacts of direct damage

Source: Hallegatte and Przyluski, 2010; Meyer et al., 2012; Hallegatte, 2014; De Groeve et al., 2014; United Nations Commission for Latin America and the Caribbean, 2016; United Nations General Assembly, 2016; GFDRR, 2017

2.3. Accounting for the cost of disasters: Countries' approaches to measuring disaster damages and losses

The assessment of countries' current practices in collecting disaster damage and loss data was first informed by a desk review, which in turn informed the development of a survey instrument that sought to collect and validate data on the one hand, complemented by additional usage questions on the other hand. With the latter the survey sought to gain an insight into the policy relevance of the gathered evidence. In the following results of both parts of the work will be summarised and discussed.

Across the OECD and partner countries, a number of efforts to account for disaster damages and losses are under way. Findings from the OECD survey show that countries increasingly move towards collecting disaster loss data, with two thirds (12 countries) of those answering the survey stating that a process to at least periodically collect disaster loss data has been put in place. In some cases where no regular process to collect disaster loss data exists, aggregate, instead of event-specific, estimates may nonetheless be made on a regular basis. Denmark, for instance, noted that Statistics Denmark and the Danish Insurance Association prepare estimates on aggregate disaster damages and losses.

Centralised versus fragmented approaches to collecting disaster damage and loss data

Central repositories bringing together disaster damage and loss data are not consistently available across countries. As Table 2.2 shows ten responding countries (Canada, Colombia, Costa Rica, France, Mexico, Poland, Slovak Republic, Slovenia, Sweden, and Turkey) have a centralised national repository for disaster loss and damage data in place, and four countries have separate repositories that include data for specific hazards in place (Austria, Finland, Japan and Switzerland). A notable good practice example for a central national all-hazards repository is Canada whose Public Safety authority maintains a comprehensive centralised database (Box 1.1 in Chapter 1). The Swiss Federal Institute for Forest, Snow and Landscape Research (WSL) on the other hand is a good practice example for a hazard-specific central national-level repository that contains comprehensive damage records for selected hazards under its mandate (Box 2.1) (OECD, 2015b; OECD, *forthcoming*).

In many countries disaster damage and loss data can be found fragmented across government agencies or levels of government. In Finland for example, each ministry is responsible for collecting disaster loss data, depending on the type of hazard under their mandate. In Austria the Federal Ministry of Interior (BMI) and the Federal Ministry of Finance (BMF) both collect disaster loss data pertaining to their mandates, but they do not feed the data into a joint repository. In Switzerland, a number of canton-level databases are available with detailed information on the disaster events.

Table 2.2. Main characteristics of national databases

Country	Host institution	Time coverage	Hazards	Thresholds for event entry	Distinction between public & private losses
Australia	No centralized national repository, but various databases	Information not provided	Natural	Information not provided	Information not provided
Austria	No centralized national repository, but sectoral repositories at different ministries	Information not provided	Natural	No thresholds	Information not provided
Canada	Public Safety Canada	From 1900	Natural & man-made	10 < casualties; 100 < people affected/injured/infected/evacuated or homeless; appeal for national/international assistance; historical significance; significant damage/interruption of normal processes	No
Colombia	Unidad Nacional para la Gestión del Riesgo de Desastres	From 1998	Natural	No thresholds	No
Costa Rica	Ministry of Economic Policy and National Planning (MIDEPLAN)	From 1988	Natural	national emergencies; plans to expand it to include all hazardous events	Yes
Finland	No centralized national repository, but sectoral repositories for different ministries	Varies by ministry (Ministry of the Interior started in 1996)	Natural & man-made	No thresholds	Yes
France	Observatoire national des risques naturels	From 1982 for cumulative losses; From 1988 for annual insured losses	Natural	abnormal intensity of a natural hazard, as established by law	Yes
Japan	No centralized national repository, but sectoral repositories for different ministries	Varies by ministry (Ministry of Land, Infrastructure, Transport and Tourism (MLIT); started the measurement of water-related losses in 1961)	Natural	No threshold	Yes
Mexico	National Disaster Prevention Centre (CENAPRED)	From 2000	Natural & man-made	N.A.	Yes
Poland	Ministry of the Interior and Administration	From 2015	Natural	1000 PLN (about 250 EUR)	Yes
Slovak Republic	Ministry of Interior and Ministry of the Environment	Information not provided	Natural	No thresholds	No
Slovenia	Administration for Civil Protection and Disaster Relief, Ministry of Defence	From 2003	Natural	When economic loss estimations at national level exceed 0.03 percent of the national budget	Information not provided
Sweden	Swedish Civil Contingencies	Information not provided	Natural	No thresholds	Yes
Switzerland	No centralized national repository, but sectoral repositories at different ministries	From 1972	Natural	Information not provided	Information not provided
Turkey	Disaster and Emergency Management Authority	From 1920	Natural & man-made	No thresholds	Information not provided

Source: Data submitted to authors as part of the 2016 OECD survey; OECD, *forthcoming*; De Groeve et al. (2014)

Box 2.1. Switzerland's floods, storms and landslide hazard database

Starting out by systematically collecting data on storm damage in Switzerland since 1972, the Federal Institute for Forest, Snow and Landscape Research (WSL) now also collects disaster loss data for damages caused by floods, debris flows, landslides as well as (since 2002) rock falls in its national repository. In total, over 20 000 entries have been generated over the years, although damage resulting from other hazards, such as avalanches, snow pressure, earthquake, lightening, hail, windstorm and drought are not noted.

The recording is based on newspaper articles for smaller events and official data from cantons and insurance companies for larger events. Damage records are relatively complete, particularly in regards to recorded insurance claims, facilitated by the circumstance that natural hazard insurance for buildings and content is mandatory throughout the country. In terms of direct loss, the WSL records show that a total of nearly CHF 14 billion in damages have been caused by floods, debris flows, landslides and rock falls in Switzerland between 1972 and 2015 (Figure 2.4), about half of which was caused by five major loss events.

Figure 2.4. Damages from floods, debris flows, landslides and rock falls (1973-2015), adjusted for inflation, based on 2015 prices

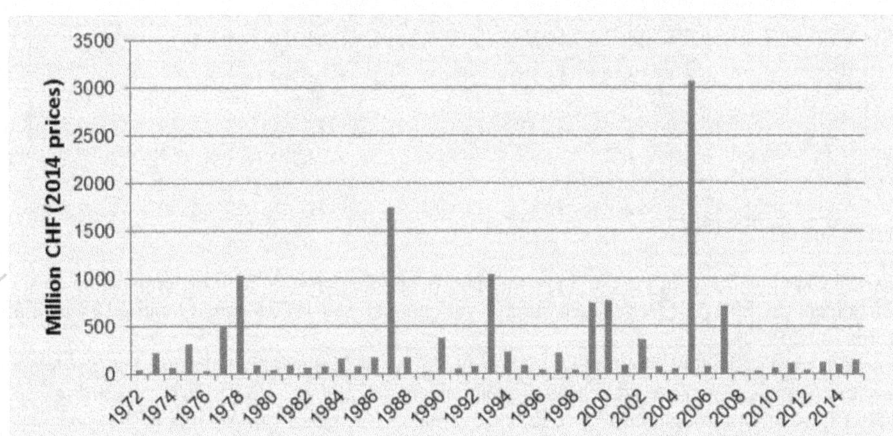

Source: FOEN (2016)

Box 2.1. Switzerland's floods, storms and landslide hazard database (*continued*)

Disaster loss data featured in the WSL repository is geo-coded, which allows a spatial analysis of damages (Figure 2.5). Results of such analyses are published yearly in the Journal "*Wasser Energie Luft*" (Water Energy Air). They are provided to official institutions on request as a broad information basis for hazard assessment.

Figure 2.5. Spatial distribution of disaster damages, 1972 – 2016

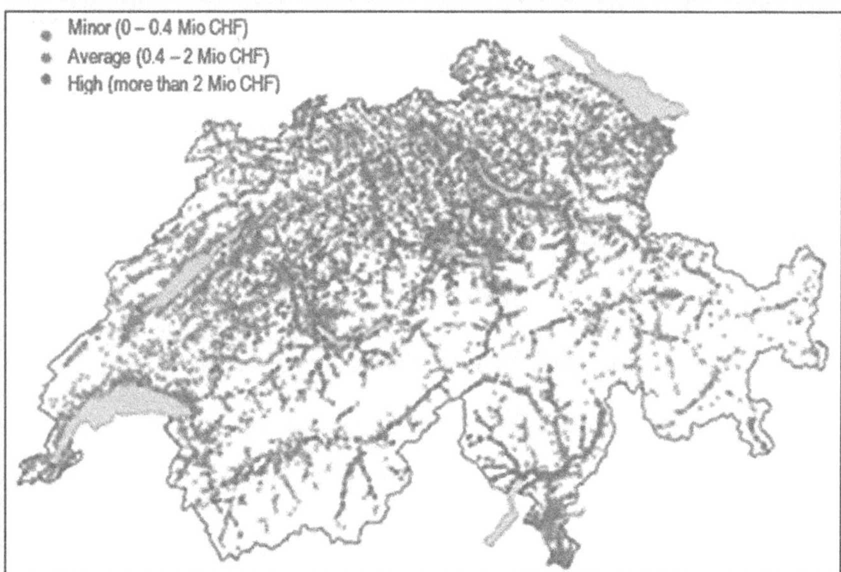

Source: WSL/FOEN (2017)

Source: Federal Institute for Forest, Snow and Landscape Research (WSL)/ Federal Office for the Environment (FOEN) (2017). Schäden durch Naturgefahren seit 1972 [Damage caused by natural hazards since 1972], www.bafu.admin.ch/bafu/de/home/themen/naturgefahren/fachinformationen/schaeden-und-lehren-aus-naturereignissen/schaeden-durch-naturgefahren-seit-1972.html; OECD (2017), Boosting Disaster Prevention through Innovative Risk Governance: Insights from Austria, France and Switzerland; Federal Office for the Environment (FOEN) (2016). Data, indicators, maps, www.bafu.admin.ch/bafu/en/home/state.html

Formal conditions for establishing disaster damage and loss repositories

A legal requirement to establish a disaster damage and loss database is useful to ensure the necessary and sustained political and resource commitment needed to support such an information collection effort. Slovenia, for example, established a legal mandate to collect disaster loss data in a centralised database as part of its emergency management processes. Slovenian legislation also includes standardised damage assessment guidelines. Austria, Japan, Spain, Switzerland and Sweden also have legislation in place that requires the collection of disaster impact data. However, those do not consistently require the collection of disaster loss data in a single national repository, nor is the allocation of funding or the creation of damage assessment standards always part of the formal frameworks (De Groeve et al., 2014; OECD, *forthcoming*).

Although legal requirements can be useful, they are not a necessary condition for establishing comprehensive data repositories. In the absence of such a legal framework, in France, for example, the significant damages caused by storm Xynthia in 2010 triggered the establishment of its national disaster loss data repository (Box 2.2) (De Groeve et al., 2014).

Box 2.2. French Observatory of Natural Risks (ONRN): collaborative public-private disaster loss data collection

Set up jointly by the Ministry of Ecology, Sustainable Development and Energy, the *Caisse centrale de réassurance* (Central Reinsurance Company, CCR) and the *Mission des sociétés d'assurances pour la connaissance et la prévention des risques naturels* (Association of French Insurance Undertakings for Natural Risk Knowledge and Reduction, MRN), and local authorities, the National Observatory of Natural Risks (*Observatoire national des risques naturels*, ONRN) is France's national repository for disaster data. Data is obtained from various sources, from government authorities over insurers to operators of critical infrastructure and utilities and researchers (Figure 2.6).

Figure 2.6. A collaborative approach to collecting disaster loss data

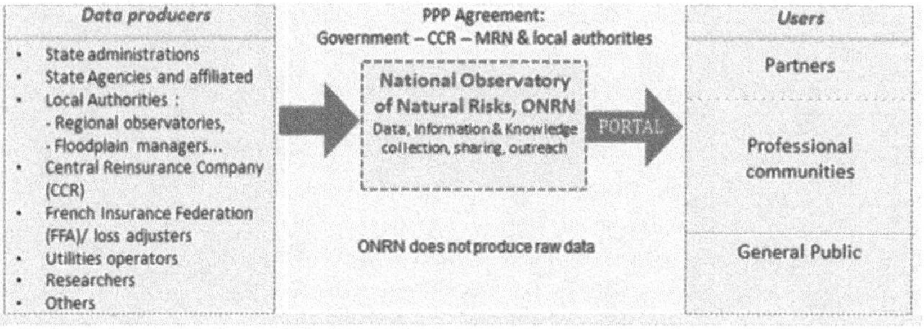

Data producers
- State administrations
- State Agencies and affiliated
- Local Authorities :
  - Regional observatories,
  - Floodplain managers...
- Central Reinsurance Company (CCR)
- French Insurance Federation (FFA)/ loss adjusters
- Utilities operators
- Researchers
- Others

PPP Agreement:
Government – CCR – MRN & local authorities

National Observatory of Natural Risks, ONRN
Data, Information & Knowledge collection, sharing, outreach

PORTAL

ONRN does not produce raw data

Users
- Partners
- Professional communities
- General Public

Source: Rothschild, 2016

Established in the aftermath of storm Xynthia in 2010 the ONRN web platform now provides a comprehensive inventory of existing public databases with easy access by topic and/or by territory to a large series of risk related information on hazards, exposure and vulnerabilities, damages and losses, and prevention projects and initiatives across the French territory. An interactive map allows a visualisation of the information at municipal scale. The earliest records date back to 1982, with more comprehensive data available since 1988, when data on insured damages and losses was increasingly added. Since 1995, data is publicly accessible online.

The establishment of the ONRN allows for the sharing of information and data collected and elaborated by different stakeholders, at central and local levels, including confidential data, and for the presentation of such information and data in a reliable, harmonised, updated and consistent manner. Increasingly, the data collected and stored in the ONRN is used to inform disaster risk management decision making. For example, when deciding on investments into disaster risk reduction measures, ONRN loss data is illustrated via the mapping tool to inform the exposure analysis. The consistent and harmonized data available through the ONRN can be used for a full range of different applications, including risk assessment, risk mitigation, emergency preparedness and financial planning.

Source: OECD (2017). Toolkit for Risk Governance, www.oecd.org/governance/toolkit-on-risk-governance/home/; Observatoire National des Risques Naturels (2017). Informations thématiques [Thematic Information], www.onrn.fr/site/rubriques/informations-thematiques.html; Rothschild, 2016, Presentation at the Joint Expert Meeting on Disaster Loss Data held at the OECD in October 2016; Nussbaum, 2016, Presentation at the Joint Expert Meeting on Disaster Loss Data held at the OECD in October 2016

Single versus multi-hazard databases

Multi-hazard disaster damage and loss databases are useful as they can facilitate an all-hazards approach to national risk assessment that helps prioritise disaster risk reduction policies at a national level and across sectors. Table 2.2 shows multi-hazard databases are not always available. Canada, Costa Rica, Colombia, France, Japan, Mexico and Slovenia are examples of countries that take an all hazards approach to collecting disaster damage and loss information, at least with regard to natural hazards. In other cases, data is only collected for specific natural hazards. In Japan, for example, different national databases are created for different purposes. Among them, the most complete national-level data available on disaster damages and losses focuses on water-related hazards. Insured damages and losses caused by major disasters are tracked by the Financial Services Agency, Japan (OECD, 2015).

Data on damages and losses caused by man-made hazards are generally not included in national level disaster damage and loss databases. Among responding countries, only Canada (see Box 1.1), Finland, Turkey and Mexico noted that information on such hazards is accounted for in the national disaster loss data collection efforts.

Thresholds and time periods covered by disaster loss data differs significantly across countries

Criteria for triggering an entry of losses in the data repository differ substantially across countries. Figure 2.7 shows that a third of responding countries have specific thresholds for loss data collection, in some of which this threshold is anchored in the national legislation or might correspond to an official disaster declaration. For example, in France, a disaster event gets recorded officially when a disaster event exceeds the "abnormal intensity" of a specific natural hazard. This threshold is set by an internal jurisprudence of the interdepartmental commission CatNat. By contrast, Canada includes all events with historical significance. Japan collects all water related disasters regardless of their scales. Finland records events only when rescue services were mobilised in the wake of the disaster. Different thresholds across countries render comparisons across them more challenging.

Figure 2.7. Thresholds for disaster event entry into the loss database

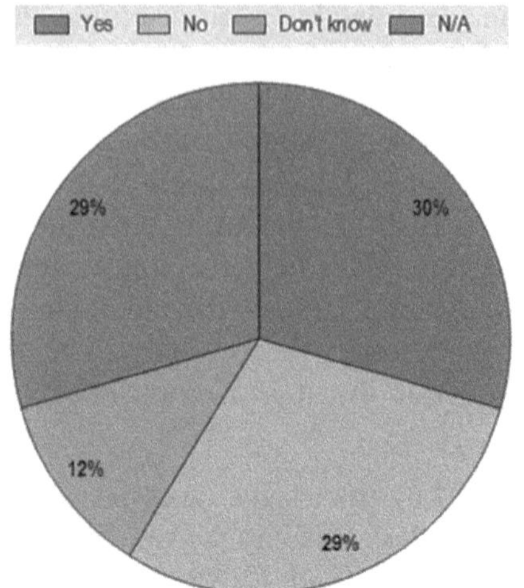

Note 1: Question asks " Does your country have a threshold (such as a certain magnitude or number of people/places affected) that must be met before economic loss data is collected on a given event?"
Note 2: N.a. refers to countries that do not have a central national body for disaster loss data collection in place.
Source: OECD Direct and Indirect economic loss collection survey

Similarly, disaster loss data is available for vastly different time periods. In Colombia, Costa Rica and Mexico, disaster loss data accounting efforts date back to 1998, 1988 and 2000 respectively (see Table 2.2). In Japan, disaster loss data for water-related hazards has been collected since 1961, while in Switzerland data collection started in 1972. Some repositories feature far older data, which usually has been obtained retroactively, e.g. via historical newspaper records or from other historical sources. Australia, for instance, noted that the oldest disaster loss data dates back to 1791, whereas in Canada the oldest entry refers to disaster events that occurred in 1900. In Turkey, the oldest entry in the Turkish database dates back to 1920. In some countries, such as Finland, not all available disaster loss data records have been fully digitalised yet.

Accessibility of disaster damage and loss information

Although the evidence base on the damages and losses caused by disasters is continuously improving across many countries, only few examples can be found that make all disaster loss data publicly accessible. Canada provides full public access to all disaster loss data collected for more than 1000 natural and man-made hazardous events stored in the repository. The online tool also allows a geospatial mapping of disaster loss data. Similarly, the French disaster loss database (Box 2.2) is publicly accessible. In other cases, disaster loss data is partially accessible for the public. In Australia, for example, publicly available disaster loss data is restricted to information on insured losses, but it can be accessed via an interactive platform that combines it with a wide array of hazard information (see Box 1.8).

2.4. Comprehensiveness of disaster damage and loss information

As outlined in the introduction to this chapter, precision is needed when it comes to understanding reported disaster damage and loss information. Different approaches and definitions exist and efforts to articulate an international standard are only just underway and hence most countries have not adopted them yet.

Evidence found across OECD and some of its partner countries shows that often the figures reported on a country level are not clear in terms of whether they include both disaster damages *and* losses, and if so what damage and loss components within them. In fact, in the cases where data on damages and losses is consistently reported, this often rests on insured losses only because insurance providers tend to have the most consistently reported figures. Table 2.3 summarises the type of information that is collected by a selected set of countries on disaster damages and losses, as reported in the OECD survey. It shows that the cost categories differ and may include public spending as a cost estimate (such as in Canada) or indeed the cost of a selected set of assets, such as houses and hospitals in France and in Finland.

Table 2.3. Economic loss data components reported in disaster databases across a selected set of countries

Country	Total costs of a disaster event	Insured losses	Damages (i.e. direct costs)	Losses (i.e. indirect costs)
Australia	n/a	yes	Estimated total cost not disaggregated	no
Canada	May include also indirect losses	yes	Yes: amount paid out by Disaster Financial Assistance Arrangements (DFAA); amount paid out by a Province/Territory or municipal governments; amount paid out by other federal institutions; amounts paid out by NGOs	No, but amount of people whose utility services (power, water, etc.) were interrupted/affected by a specific event is specified
Colombia	Only direct losses	n/a	Yes: Assistance provided via the National Disaster Fund (*Fondo Nacional De Calamidades*)	no
Finland	May include also indirect losses	n/a	Yes: Houses and hospitals	sometimes
France	May include also indirect losses	yes	Yes: Houses and hospitals	sometimes
Japan	May include also indirect losses (for water-related disasters)	no (for water-related disasters)	1) estimated costs of damage to assets owned by fisherman and farmers 2) damages to agricultural products 3) Damages to residential Properties; 4) Emergency cost of households 5) Damaged Business Assets; 6) Emergency costs of businesses	yes: losses due to water-related public services and utilities; losses due to business suspension
Mexico	May include also indirect losses	n/a	Yes: Buildings (houses, schools, hospitals) collapsed/damaged; Damaged Agricultural Area in ha; Km of roads damaged.	sometimes
Norway	n/a	yes	n/a	n/a
Sweden	Only direct losses	yes	Yes: Direct losses to houses, commercial and industrial facilities, critical infrastructure, environment damaged/destroyed; number of critical infrastructure damaged (education and health facilities, security services), number of tourist infrastructure damaged	n/a
Turkey	Only direct losses	n/a	Yes: Buildings collapsed/damaged; Damaged Agricultural Area; Cattle Loss	no

Source: OECD Direct and Indirect economic loss collection survey

The answers to the OECD complementary survey questions also confirm that the distinction between direct and indirect economic losses (or disaster damage and losses) may not be made consistently (Figure 2.8). In some countries that report accounting for indirect losses this may only be recorded on a case-by-case basis or for selected hazards only, such as in Japan, where this is only done for water-related hazards (Box 1.2). In Finland, an estimation of indirect loss is typically conducted for major disaster events. France, Costa Rica and Mexico also note that disaster loss data accounts occasionally include indirect losses. Even where data on indirect loss is collected, methodologies used to calculate them differ, limiting conclusiveness and comparability of such assessments.

Figure 2.8. Direct and indirect economic losses accounted separately

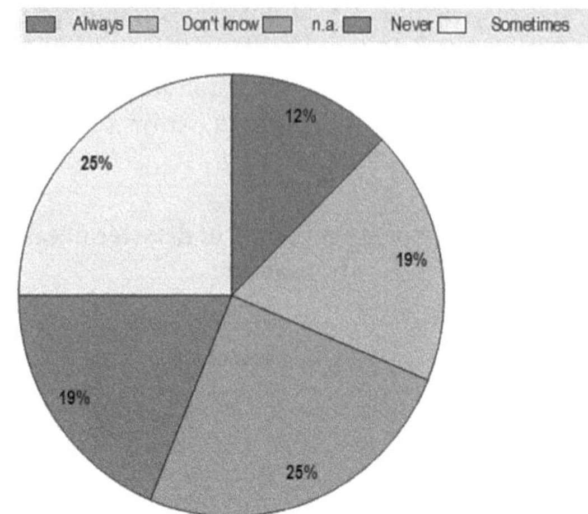

Note 1: Question asks: "Does your country separately account for direct and indirect economic losses?".
Note 2: N.a. refers to countries that do not have a central national body for disaster loss data collection in place.
Source: OECD Direct and Indirect economic loss collection survey

As mentioned in the introduction to this chapter, apart from direct and indirect costs, there is sometimes another cost category distinguished, which is the one on intangible costs. This is a cost category that is difficult to measure, as no market prices are readily available to calculate them. Costs in this category are for example the results of damages to the environment or to cultural heritage. This cost category is perhaps the least considered in systematic disaster damage and loss accounting. Approaches, such as the damage assessment for cultural heritage sites, suggested by UNESCO, could be a useful starting point in putting together loss estimates for such intangible costs (Box 2.3).

Box 2.3. Accounting for damages to cultural assets: the UNESCO approach

Examples of intangible damages include the destruction or damage of cultural and historical assets, the cost of which may go beyond material damage. During the 2016 earthquake in central Italy, for instance, multiple historic buildings were destroyed, including the San Benedetto basilica in Norcia and the 15th-century church of Sant'Agostino.

In recognition of the potential negative impact that disasters may have on world heritage, the United Nations Educational, Scientific and Cultural Organization (UNESCO) in 2010 published a manual that should assist the systematic accounting of damages to cultural assets. The manual provides guidance for the damage assessment process. It suggests planning damage assessments prior to disasters by collecting information regarding the heritage site that is often difficult and time intensive to collect. In the absence of such information at the time of assessing disaster damage, this may pose a serious impediment.

Source: The Guardian, 2016; United Nations Educational, Scientific and Cultural Organization (2010). Managing Disaster Risks for World Heritage, http://whc.unesco.org/en/managing-disaster-risks/

Distributional disaster impacts: differentiating costs by type of actor that incurs them

Differentiating disaster damages and losses by the type of actor that incurs them, such as a private household, a business, or a public agency, is useful for many purposes. It can support policy makers in estimating the amount of contingent government liabilities arising from an obligation or commitment to provide post-disaster assistance or to pay for the rehabilitation and recovery for its own assets. Information on the distributional impacts by actors enables more targeted disaster risk communication and policies that aim at reducing losses incurred by different actors over time. Aggregated disaster loss figures may make it easy to assume that "others" must have faced the brunt of disaster losses, whereas disaggregated data illustrates where disaster damages and losses are actually accrued. If communicated adequately towards households and businesses, such disaggregated data can be useful to boost uptake of self-protection and risk transfer measures.

Many national loss estimation methodologies do not differentiate whether losses are accrued by public authorities or by private actors (Figure 2.9). Some examples nevertheless exist:

- In the Czech Republic, where the central government reimburses sub-national expenditure spent on the recovery of assets, sub-national governments are obliged to submit separate estimates of both public and private damages incurred to the Ministry of Finance within seven days after the declared end of the emergency (OECD, 2015).
- In France, disaster loss data collection goes hand in hand with the public-private CatNat insurance scheme, which is the main mechanism for post-disaster compensation.
- In Finland, disaster loss data is used to inform post-disaster compensation, as foreseen by the Act on Compensation for Environmental Damage. Increasingly however, post-disaster compensation responsibilities in Finland are shifted to

private insurance companies, which in the future may have an impact of disaster loss data disaggregation practices (BASE, 2016).

- In Mexico, the differentiation is made in line with post-disaster compensation and assistance provided via the Fund for Natural Disasters (*Fondo de Desastres Naturales*, FONDEN). As the central government only provides financial post-disaster assistance to low income households and agricultural producers without insurance (as well as to sub-national governments), disaster loss data tends to be only available for compensation and recovery payments made to these categories. Consequently, difficulties in regards to obtaining information on overall private sector damages outside the low-income span have been noted.
- In Japan water-related disaster damages and losses are by default disaggregated by ownership. Municipal governments are charged with assessing damages to private properties, while damages to public works and services are predominantly assessed by prefectural governments, integrating information provided by municipal governments (Box 1.2).

Figure 2.9. Distinction between publicly and privately accrued economic losses

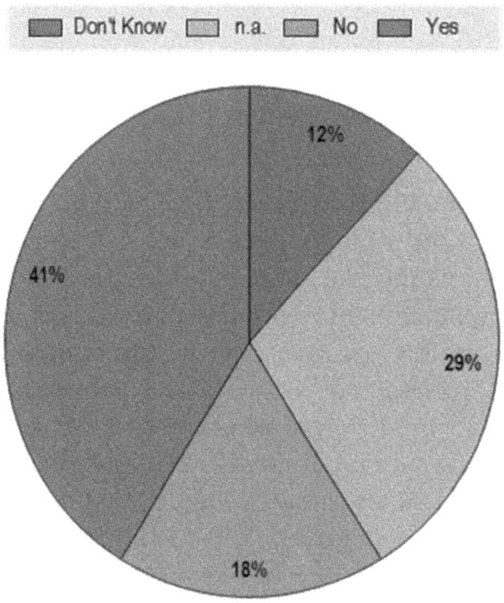

Note 1: Question asks "Does your country distinguish between publicly and privately accrued economic losses?"
Note 2: N.a. refers to countries that do not have a central national body for disaster loss data collection in place.
Source: OECD Direct and Indirect economic loss collection survey

Comparability of existing national level disaster damage and loss data

Cross-country comparability of disaster damage and loss data remains a challenge. The reviewed country level information shows although definitions exist for what constitutes direct physical impacts and to estimate their monetary value such as for affected buildings, agricultural assets and civil infrastructure, countries do not consistently apply these methods when assessing damages after disaster events. Losses, in the sense of indirect costs, are even less consistently assessed and reported. These include costs emanating from the interruption of activities at business and household levels, transport interruption or interruption of lifelines. More intangible costs such as the impact on health or the environment are hardly ever accounted for due to difficulties in monetisation.

Several international disaster statistics repositories exist that are working to improve the quality of disaster information and to increase its comparability across countries. Table 2.4 lists four of the more comprehensive sets of data that can be found and that are accessible online. Whereas EM-DAT is maintained by the Centre for the Epidemiology of Disasters at the University of Louvain, the NatCat Service and Sigma are financed and managed by the private sector, in this case reinsurance providers. In terms of disaster damages and losses reported and accessible by events, EM-DAT is among the most complete repositories that can be found (Box 2.4).

International data repositories are reliant on efforts undertaken by national governments; however they have employed alternative sourcing of information in the absence of faster progress and engagement by national governments. In itself these efforts can be useful, because if consistently sourced over time at least trends analyses can be conducted, as shown in the introductory Figures 2.1 and 2.2 of this chapter. It would of course be desirable to replace the coarse information in the long-run with more comprehensive government-validated data. International data repositories have been a major force in driving national efforts as they incentivise countries' willingness to improve available records.

Box 2.4. The international Emergency Events Database (EM-DAT): A global multi-hazard disaster repository

The international Emergency Events Database (EM-DAT) is a publicly accessible global multi-hazard database provided by the Centre for Research on the Epidemiology of Disasters at Louvain University. The database features data on the date and location of disaster events, which allows a mapping of events, as well as information on disasters' socio-economic impact. This includes the number of deaths caused by the event, the number of injured and homeless and the number of those affected by the disaster. In addition, damage estimations are included for 45 % of disaster events registered in OECD countries for the period 1995-2015.

Data is compiled from various sources including UN bodies, governmental and non-governmental agencies, insurance companies, research institutes and press agencies. To increase the reliability of the data, at least two sources need to report the disaster's occurrence in terms of impact data. Where featured, the total damage (in '000 US$ current value) seeks to describe the estimated value of all damages and economic losses directly or indirectly related to the disaster, excluding reconstruction costs. As damage and loss data is obtained from various sources, rather than measured by EM-DAT, the comparability of damage data is not guaranteed.

Despite the missing values and differing approaches to measuring the economic impact of disasters across countries and sources, the database allows cross-country comparisons. This can be useful for vulnerability assessments and enables policymakers to identify resilience gaps linked to the disaster types that are most common and impactful in a given country. Despite the potential for cross-country comparisons and vulnerability assessments, results from the 2016 OECD Survey showed that only very few countries use the available international databases.

Source: EM-DAT: CRED/OFDA International Disaster Database (2017), www.emdat.be

Table 2.4. Major international (ex-post) economic loss databases and main characteristics

Name of database	Location coverage	Hazard coverage	Events covered since	Threshold levels	Variables covered	Total economic loss calculation	Source of information for hazards and losses
EM-DAT	World-wide	All hazards (natural, technological)	1900 (about 18,000 disasters)	10 < casualties; 100 < affected; declaration of state of emergency; call for intern. assistance	Casualties, affected (injured, homeless, affected), estimated damage	Physical quantification: no Direct and indirect losses but does not include reconstruction costs (replacement costs for assets); direct losses include damage to infrastructure, crops, housing and indirect include loss of revenue, unemployment, market destabilisation	United Nations, Governments, International Federation of the Red Cross, World Bank, Re-Insurers, media and other related institutions
DesInventar	45 countries	All hazards (natural, socio-natural or technological)	Country-dependent	Only events that generated 'some kind of impact'	Casualties, affected (wounded, sick, relocated, evacuated, etc.); loss value, infrastructure impacts	Physical quantification: yes Direct tangible costs only	Newspapers; official government or public agencies' reports
Natcat-SERVICE (MunichRe)	World-wide	Natural hazards	1980 (about 28,000 disasters)	Some socio-economic impact; small-scale property damage or 1-9 fatalities	Insured losses; total losses; injured; infrastructure areas and industries affected	Physical quantification: yes Partly relies on total economic loss figures provided by governments, multilateral finance institutions; if former is unavailable insured losses are extrapolated via insurance density of affected region based on type of event and exposure of affected region; if insured losses are not available, extrapolations are based on event type, exposure of affected region, population density and information on physical damages	Insurance industry, research organisations, government, UN, EU, NGOs, meteorological services, news agencies
Sigma (SwissRe)	World-wide	All hazards (natural and man-made)	1970 (about 9,000 disasters)	20< casualties; 50< injured; 2000< homeless; total losses < USD 91,1 million	Casualties; missing; injured; homeless; insured losses (claims); total losses	Physical quantification: yes Insured plus uninsured losses (includes property and business interruption of insured losses and excludes liability and life insurance); total losses include financial losses due to damage to buildings, infrastructure, vehicles and other assets, business interruption; insured losses are gross of reinsurance; total losses do not include indirect financial losses (loss of earnings by suppliers, estimated shortfall in GDP, loss of reputation or quality of life impacts)	Newspapers, direct insurance and reinsurance periodicals, specialist publications and reports from insurers and reinsurers

2.5. Estimating disaster damages and losses ex-ante

Disaster damage and losses can be identified and recorded after or before disasters occur. In contrast to ex-post assessments discussed earlier in this chapter, ex-ante loss estimations are used to calculate the potential impact of a certain type and severity of a future disaster on the affected population and economy. Box 2.5 provides an example for how this has been done in the case of a major flood potentially affecting the metropolitan area of Paris in France.

Ex-ante loss assessments can help policy makers to understand future damage potential and take more informed strategic positions. On the one hand, results from such loss estimations may be useful for informing a comprehensive and evidence-based assessment of the overall amount of resources to be invested in disaster risk reduction measures. On the other hand they can inform a countries' expected amount of government disaster related contingent liabilities, their potential impact on a country's overall public finances and fiscal position (Box 2.6).

Box 2.5. Modelling the macro-economic impacts of a major Seine flood

In France, the OECD calculated the macro-economic impact of three flood scenarios based on the 100-year flood of 1910. For this purpose, a hybrid approach was developed, combining modelling of direct losses, assessment of the impacts connected with the interruption of critical networks and macroeconomic modelling.

With regards to the macro-economic impact, a dynamic general equilibrium model was developed to assess the indirect effects on growth, employment and public finances and to incorporate non-linear effects. A national model enabled to represent the impact dynamically in the short, medium and longer term. The incorporation of the specific features of the compensation funding linked to the French natural catastrophe insurance system, CatNat, also made it possible to assess the impact on the public debt and to test various scenarios in the budget response to such a catastrophe. According to the scenarios (Figure 2.10), the reduction in GDP over five years has been estimated at EUR 1.5 to 58.5 billion, i.e. a consolidated total reduction of 0.1 to 3 percent. The resulting contraction in business activity could have a significant effect on the demand for labour; up to 400,000 jobs could be lost in the worst case scenario. Even if a rebound in business activity could rapidly reduce some of these effects after a year, the harmful consequences of a major Seine flood could be felt over the medium to long term and weigh on public finances. In the case where the impact exceeds the reserves available through the national catastrophe compensation regime CatNat and the Central Reinsurance Fund (*Caisse Centrale de Réassurance*, CCR), the State could be called on to fully assume its role of ultimate guarantor.

Box 2.5. Modelling the macro-economic impacts of a major Seine flood *(continued)*

Figure 2.10. Macro-economic impact of a flood scenario over 5 years (in %)

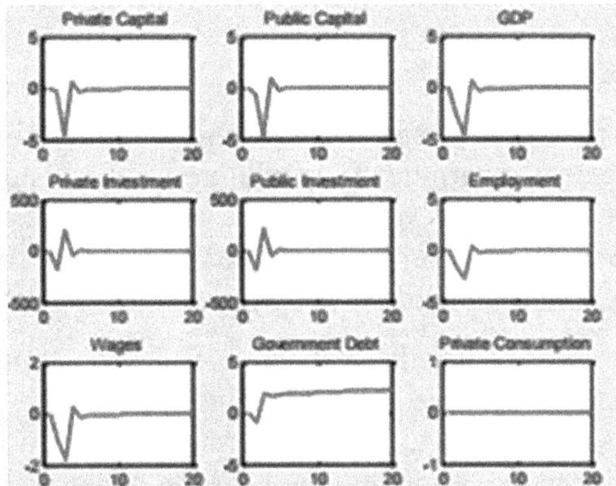

Note: These charts show the variation of the different parameters as a percentage of the initial state as a function of time with the quarterly measurement. The flood occurred during the first quarter. The flood scenario represented S3 corresponds to a flood with the same water-height as the 1910 one, with a flow 15percent greater.
Source: OECD (2014b)

Source: OECD (2014b). Seine Basin, Île-de-France, 2014: Resilience to Major Floods, OECD Publishing, Paris, http://dx.doi.org/10.1787/19934106

Box 2.6. The link between disaster related contingent liabilities, public finances and fiscal risks

Contingent liabilities refer to (government) obligations that are triggered when a potential, but uncertain future event occurs. Once a disaster event occurred contingent liabilities turn into actual expenditures.

A disaster may have significant impact on **public finances**, in that the government obligations cause changes in government expenditures and revenues. Particularly in case of a major disaster the expenditures resulting from such liabilities may cause an increase in public debt and, depending on their size, create a fiscal risk to government finances, especially if a government has not made ex-ante provisions to meet these possible costs.

Fiscal risks describe changes in the expected fiscal outcomes as outlined in an economy's annual budget or forecasting documents. Fiscal risks may have positive or negative effects on the annual budget. While governments tend to foresee and arrange for positive fiscal risks with relative accuracy, the possible negative impact of fiscal risks is often underestimated. Governments may face a various types of fiscal risks, ranging from various shocks to macroeconomic variables to the realization of contingent liabilities, such as in the event of disasters. Other fiscal risks can include government bailouts for troubled financial institutions and state-owned enterprises and private corporations, demands for government compensation, as well as subnational governments that require financial support from the central government.

Source: OECD, *forthcoming*

Generally speaking, three elements are usually combined to derive ex-ante loss estimations: first, determining the conditions of a hazard; second, estimating the number and value of exposed assets; and, third, using a loss estimation method to assess the probability of damage to the exposed assets based on the hazard conditions. While the elements differ depending on the hazard being studied, the base construction remains the same. An overview of the most common models in use is provided in Annex B

Ex-ante loss estimation models have been applied across a number of OECD countries and have informed policy decisions in countries' risk management (OECD, *forthcoming*):

- In New Zealand the government carried out a one-off study to understand the worst case impact a major disaster could have for the central government. The 2010 study modelled the fiscal impact of a 7.8 magnitude earthquake affecting its capital Wellington showing an estimated government contingent liability of USD 11 billion to finance response and recovery for three consecutive years following the modelled earthquake scenario. The Canterbury earthquakes proved this study useful as the actual fiscal costs came close to the estimates established in the study's model.
- In an effort to give an outlook on the changes to the government's future disaster related contingent liabilities (in complement to the exercise of accounting for liabilities on the basis of past commitments through the Natural Disaster Relief and Recovery Arrangements (NDRRA) Australia's Productivity Commission, the Australian Government's independent research and advisory body, makes longer term projections, one of which expects the annual costs of disasters to increase from up to USD 11.1 billion in 2018 to USD 11.5 billion by 2023.

- Mexico has developed sophisticated probabilistic models to evaluate the scale of future disasters threatening the economy. To do so, information on the past negative impacts of natural hazards was combined with data collected in the inventory of public assets, supplied by all federal government departments. Models were developed and calibrated for earthquakes and tropical cyclones. The R-FONDEN tool was developed, which provides estimates for individual scenarios or for the entire catalogue of modelled events at any geographic zone. The results from these probabilistic simulations have been used in the design of the country's main disaster risk financing mechanism, the Fund for Natural Disasters (*Fondo de Desastres Naturales*, FONDEN), which includes both provisions for the post-disaster recovery of public infrastructure and for investments in disaster risk reduction (OECD, 2013; OECD, 2015).
- As part of the development of a national seismic profile, the Ministry of Economics and Finance in Peru estimated the exposed value of state assets to calculate the maximum probable loss of a return period for a 1000-year event at USD 2.6 billion.

2.6. Discussion of results

This chapter provided an overview of ongoing country efforts on collecting disaster damage and loss data. The overview is many ways incomplete, as considerable efforts for improving or gathering existing country level data are ongoing and in that the review has had to rely on the responses we received from a set, instead of all, OECD and some of its partner countries. Despite these limitations, some key findings can be drawn out:

- Data on disaster damages and losses is already collected across many countries.
- In many countries formal frameworks have been established that determine the processes for collecting and storing disaster impact information. Even in the absence of such formal arrangements, country initiatives, sometimes provoked by the experience of major disasters, have led to the establishment of institutions and processes for collecting disaster impact data.
- There is value in centralising disaster impact data, bringing together information on multiple hazards from across agencies and levels of government. Country practices that take an ambitious and integrated approach to collecting and centralising data can use this information for informing national risk assessments and for setting strategic priorities for the management of multiple prevailing risks.
- The distinction between disaster damages (i.e. direct costs) and disaster losses (i.e. indirect costs) remains blurred and in most national and international data repositories it is not clear what the reported cost figures actually entail.
- Disaster damages to cultural heritage sites, the environment or public health are amongst the least studied and most difficult to evaluate disaster impacts.
- Ex-ante loss estimation methods have been increasingly established and taken up by a number of countries' policy makers to inform strategic policy decisions. The better the ex-post reporting on disaster damages and losses is, the more robust will ex-ante loss assessments become.
- International guidance on disaster damage and loss collection methods can strengthen national level efforts as well as international comparability. The latter will also enable the measurement of progress towards achieving global targets and indicators such as under the Sendai Framework for Disaster Risk Reduction or the Sustainable Development Goals.

Notes

[1] The online OECD survey was filled out by 17 countries (Australia, Austria, Canada, Colombia, Costa Rica, Denmark, Estonia, Finland, France, Japan, Israel, Mexico, Norway, Poland, Slovak Republic, Sweden, and Turkey). Annex B provides the survey and the full list of names of the responding institution in each country.

[2] Annex B. More information on the workshops and presentation material can be found under the following links: http://www.oecd.org/gov/risk/joint-expert-meeting-on-disaster-loss-data.htm; http://www.oecd.org/gov/risk/improving-the-evidence-base-on-the-costs-of-disasters.htm

References

Bottom-up Climate Adaptation Strategies towards a sustainable Europe (BASE) (2016). Shifting responsibilities for flood damages in Finland, http://base-adaptation.eu/shifting-responsibilities-flood-damages-finland

Colombia Ministry of Finance and Public Credit (2011). Contingent Liabilities: The Colombian Experience. http://treasury.worldbank.org/bdm/pdf/Contingent_Liabilities_Colombian_Experience.pdf

De Groeve, T., Poljansek, K., Ehrlich, D. and C. Corbane (2014). Current status and Best Practices for Disaster Loss Data recording in EU Member States. JRC Scientific and Policy Reports, European Commission.

Federal Institute for Forest, Snow and Landscape Research (WSL)/ Federal Office for the Environment (FOEN) (2017). Schäden durch Naturgefahren seit 1972 [Damage caused by natural hazards sinec 1972], https://www.bafu.admin.ch/bafu/de/home/themen/naturgefahren/fachinformationen/schaeden-und-lehren-aus-naturereignissen/schaeden-durch-naturgefahren-seit-1972.html;

Federal Office for the Environment (FOEN) (2016). Data, indicators, maps, https://www.bafu.admin.ch/bafu/en/home/state.html

Global Facility for Disaster Reduction and Recovery (GFDRR), 2017. Damage and Loss Assessment (DaLA) Methodology, www.gfdrr.org/damage-loss-and-needs-assessment-tools-andmethodology

Hallegatte, S. (2014). Economic Resilience. Definition and Measurement. Policy Research Working Paper 6852, The World Bank

Hallegatte, S. and V. Przyluski (2010).The Economics of Natural Disasters. Concepts and Methods, Policy Research Working Paper 5507, The World Bank, https://openknowledge.worldbank.org/handle/10986/3991

Meyer, V., Becker, N., Markantonis, V. and R. Schwarze (2012).Costs of Natural Hazards – A Synthesis. Report prepared by ConHaz Consortium under EC Seventh Framework Programme, Contract 244159

Nussbaum, R. (2016). Presentation at the Joint Expert Meeting on Disaster Loss Data held at the OECD, Paris, www.slideshare.net/OECD-GOV/mrn-french-experience-in-econ-loss-accounting-roland-nussbaum

Observatoire National des Risques Naturels (2017). Informations thématiques [Thematic Information], www.onrn.fr/site/rubriques/informations-thematiques.html

OECD (2013). Review of the Mexican National Civil Protection System, OECD Publishing, Paris, http://dx.doi.org/10.1787/9789264192294-en

OECD (2015). Disaster Risk Financing: A global survey of practices and challenges, OECD Publishing, Paris, www.oecd.org/publications/disaster-risk-financing-9789264234246-en.htm

OECD (2017). Toolkit for Risk Governance, www.oecd.org/governance/toolkit-on-risk-governance/home/

OECD (*forthcoming*), Managing Disaster Related Contingent Liabilities in Public Finance Frameworks – Preliminary Findings from selected economies, Draft Report, OECD Publishing, Paris

Rothschild, E. (2016). Presentation at the Joint Expert Meeting on Disaster Loss Data held at the OECD, Paris, www.slideshare.net/OECD-GOV/nationals-view-on-evidencebased-assessment-of-the-sendai-indicators-france-elsa-rothschild-ccr

UNESCO (2010). Managing Disaster Risks for World Heritage, United Nations Educational, Scientific and Cultural Organization, http://whc.unesco.org/en/managing-disaster-risks/

United Nations General Assembly (2016). Report of the open-ended intergovernmental expert working group on indicators and terminology relating to disaster risk reduction, www.preventionweb.net/files/50683_oiewgreportenglish.pdf

3. Public expenditures for disaster risk management: Assessing the state of the art

Information on public expenditure is an important element for effective and efficient resource allocation decisions in disaster risk reduction. For policy makers to understand how effectively their invested resources acted towards reducing losses of comparable disasters over time, knowledge on how much was spent on different measures is crucial. This chapter first introduces the value and approaches to identifying public expenditures for disaster risk management. It then outlines and discusses why country practices in that regard have been limited to a few expenditure reviews, existing evidence for which will be presented as well.

3.1. Introduction

The measurement of the costs of disasters consists of two main components: disaster losses on the one hand and disaster risk management expenditures on the other. For effective disaster risk management policy making it is essential to understand and record the damages and losses comparable disasters cause over time, and in contrast, to know how much resources were engaged to contain or reduce them. Only if both components are well understood, can policy makers assess how effectively they are managing disasters over time. In line with this, the OECD Recommendation on the Governance of Critical Risks (OECD, 2014) calls on its Adherents to adopt broad frameworks for assessing risk-related expenditures. These frameworks should record the expenditures at national and local level, to the extent possible.

While Chapter 2 of this report focused on the rationale and the methods for measuring disaster losses, providing a summary of the progress and current practices to collect this information across OECD and some partner countries, this chapter complements the discussion by focussing on disaster risk management expenditure. As will be shown, this aspect of the measurement work in disaster risk management has received considerably less attention by policy makers, and experts alike, and hence the evidence base to review progress and practices in this regard across OECD and partner countries is comparatively smaller. The implications and policy conclusions, however, may not be any less important.

This chapter draws on information that was collected as part of the same multi-annual project of the OECD High Level Risk Forum on Assessing the Costs of Disasters that Chapter 2 drew on. Results from the survey are presented along with information gathered through desk reviews and during expert meetings held at the OECD. The objective of this chapter is to discuss the rationale of systematically collecting expenditure information on disaster risk management as well as to summarise the current country practices found on recording such expenditure. An outlook and recommendations for future work will be provided in the concluding chapter 4 of this report.

3.2. Expenditure for disaster risk management – what measures are needed?

Disaster risk management (DRM) expenditure by the government emanates from engagements of public resources both before a disaster occurs as well as after, in response to a disaster. While governments are not the only entity to engage resources for managing disasters, they frequently shoulder a large share of the costs, especially in terms of investments into structural measures to prevent disasters and for disaster recovery and compensation in countries where insurance coverage is limited. Such costs are for example due to the obligation to restore public assets and services, but they may also include implicit contingent liabilities, i.e. unanticipated expenditures that are not budgeted for but for which there is some moral expectation that they will be made (Gamper et al., 2017). Governments also engage resources for emergency preparedness and response ahead of the occurrence of disasters, to enable quick and efficient disaster response.

Table 3.1 provides a non-exhaustive overview of the major types of activities for which public resources are spent in disaster risk management as well as the type of costs that are most often encountered. It shows that governments engage resources ex-ante of disasters for activities such as hazard and risk assessments and land-use planning as well as the investments in physical risk reduction measures, but also resources that aim at increasing a country's emergency preparedness capacity through the development of crisis management plans, early warning systems or emergency supply management.

Table 3.1. Public expenditure for disaster risk management: Overview of cost categories and types

	Sub-category
I. Disaster Risk Prevention and Mitigation	I.1 Strategic Planning
	I.2 Hazard Identification and Assessment
	I.3 Risk/Hazard Mapping
	I.4 Land-use Planning
	I.5 Planning, Developing and Constructing of Protective Infrastructure
	I.6 Prevention measures for the existing built environment (houses, etc.)
	I.7 Prevention measures for critical infrastructure
	I.8 Risk awareness and communication activities
	I.9 Risk Transfer Investments by the Public Sector
	I.10 Other public investments in ex-ante/ex-post financial arrangements (subsidies for reconstruction loans, guarantees for federal compensation funds, subsidies for insurance schemes)
II. Disaster/ Emergency Preparedness	II.1 Development of Crisis Management Plans
	II.2 Early Warning Systems Development, Construction and Management
	II.3 Evacuation Planning and Management
	II.4 Emergency Supply Management
	II.5 Emergency Preparedness/Crisis Management Exercises
	III.1 Emergency Supplies
	II.1 Development of Crisis Management Plans
	II.2 Early Warning Systems Development, Construction and Management
	II.3 Evacuation Planning and Management
	II.4 Emergency Supply Management
	II.5 Emergency Preparedness/Crisis Management Exercises
III. Disaster/Emergency Response	III.1 Emergency Supplies
	III.2 Assistance Packages to affected regions, households etc.
	III.3 Payments to NGO's and other emergency support agencies
	III.4 Expenditure related to immediate response to public service disruption (energy and water supply, transport, etc.)
	III.5 Search and rescue operations
	III.1 Emergency Supplies
IV. Post-Disaster Rehabilitation and Reconstruction	IV.1 Rehabilitation of public infrastructure
	IV.2 Reconstruction of public infrastructure
	V. Financial assistance and compensation in support of disaster recovery to households
	VI. Financial assistance and compensation in support of disaster recovery to businesses
	IV.1 Rehabilitation of public infrastructure

Identifying and systematically recording disaster risk management expenditure is challenging for several reasons:

- Disaster risk related expenditures entail spending that is usually not thematically reported in public accounts or budgets.
- Expenditure is undertaken by different sectors of the government, such as environment, transport, communications or civil protection departments. Each sector may have a different approach to distinguishing or recording expenditure, and may not always distinguish expenditure that contributes to disaster risk

management. Each sector may have their own way of distinguishing hazards and types of risk reduction investment (e.g. prevention, preparedness, rehabilitation).

- Subnational levels of government often shoulder substantial parts of the costs of disasters, both in terms of investments made prior to disasters to reduce their negative impacts and in terms of post-disaster recovery spending.

Expenditure may be embedded, i.e. expenditure for a project may only partially pertain to disaster risk reduction and may thus be very difficult to identify or never even get recorded as such. The construction of a dam might first and foremost serve the purpose of generating electricity, and only indirectly serve as a flood control measure. Expenditure accounts are essentially the result of budgeting processes, i.e. the decision making process through which the level of spending (and revenue generation) in public administration is set. The process is influenced not only by public governments and agencies, but also non-governmental organisations (such as the private sector). Budgeting processes differ largely across and within countries, depending on the political as well as the fiscal or federal system countries have adopted. Budgeting processes may be relatively transparent and open (even including participatory elements by citizens) and traceable for anyone interested, or taking place behind closed doors, whereby only the final outcome is made public. All those elements create a complex environment where information on disaster risk management expenditure is situated and where it needs to be extracted from.

Generally speaking, there is little academic guidance available on how to carry out public expenditure reviews or use standard methodologies to establish cross-country comparisons. Sectoral expenditure reviews can be conducted relatively easily within one country. Establishing comparative expenditure categories for one sector across countries poses a greater challenge and cross-sectoral assessments within and across countries even more so. Nevertheless, establishing a cross-country database containing such expenditure information can help inform policy makers about good practices and benchmarks, and could give a comparative perspective to their own internal spending and prioritisation.

Accounting for public spending provides a large, but not a complete picture of all resources engaged to manage disaster risks. To be fully comprehensive such an expenditure assessment would need to also include private spending on disaster risk management. Information on private investments in disaster risk reduction is however hard to obtain, as it sits with businesses and households or NGOs, making it very challenging to obtain this data in a systematic way.

In light of these constraints, the OECD work on disaster risk management expenditures sought to take account of and identify approaches that countries have taken to collect public disaster risk management expenditure, and to the extent feasible, assess the impact this information had on policy decisions. The following section provides an overview of the results this facts gathering work obtained through OECD wide surveys as well as complementary desk research.

3.3. Overview of country practices collecting disaster risk management expenditure information

To take stock of current country practices with regard to information on disaster risk management expenditure, this section draws on three main sources of information: (i) the 2016 OECD survey on the "Cost of Disasters"[1]; (ii) two OECD expert workshops held in 2014 and 2016 on the "Cost of Disasters"[2]; and (iii) complementary desk research.

Very few countries know the exact amount of public resources they engage to manage disaster risks in their countries. The 2016 OECD survey showed that less than half of responding countries collect information on disaster risk management expenditure (Figure 3.1), and only half of those countries reporting to collect such information, notably France, Turkey, Japan, Colombia and Austria, were able to provide an approximate yearly expenditure figures.

Figure 3.1. Disaster risk management expenditures collection

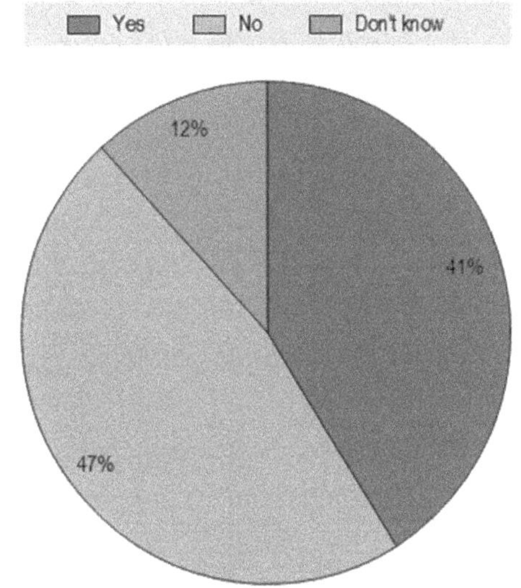

Note: Question asks "Does your country collect information on disaster risk management expenditure?"
Source: OECD Direct and Indirect economic loss collection survey.

In complement to the OECD survey, only a limited number of more in-depth expenditure reviews on disaster risk management across OECD and some of its partner countries were identifiable. Table 3.2 provides an overview of practices for which more detailed information could be obtained on the nature of such reviews.

Regular national level disaster risk management expenditure reviews are rare. Of the limited number of country reviews that were identified through the OECD information collection efforts on disaster risk management expenditure, almost all examples are the result of a one-time project or programme set-up to retrieve this information from sectoral budgets across relevant sectors and, sometimes, including expenditure from different levels of government. For instance, in Switzerland, the Swiss National Platform for Natural Hazards conducted a onetime spending survey for disaster risk management, while in France the General Commission for Sustainable Development developed a onetime overview of ex-ante disaster risk management expenditure. Expenditures made at subnational levels are often not reflected. The OECD review found only one national example where disaster risk management expenditures are regularly collected and officially reported, which was Japan.

The major obstacle to collecting expenditure information on a regular basis lies in the fact that disaster risk management does not exist as an official expenditure category in public accounts, but remains "embedded" in differently reported expenditure categories across national level agencies and different government levels.

Depending on their objectives, disaster risk management expenditure reviews distinguish resources spent ex-ante of disasters in disaster preparedness and other disaster risk reduction efforts as well as ex-post disaster recovery and reconstruction. Different reviews include different types of hazards, and as a consequence some are able to identify expenditure by different hazard types. Table 3.2 provides an overview of the types of categories that are distinguished in the reviewed disaster risk management expenditure assessments.

Table 3.2. Existing national expenditure frameworks

		Australia	Austria	France	Japan	Colombia	Mexico	Switzerland	United States of America
Classification	**Institutions**	N/A	Yes	Yes	No	Yes	Yes	Yes	N/A
	Hazard	No	No	Yes (only national level)	No	No	No	Yes	No
	Risk management cycle (functions)	Yes	No	No (only prevention and mitigation)	Yes	No, but by HFA Priorities, Plan and Non-plan	No, but by HFA Priorities, Plan and Non-plan	Yes	Yes
	Other	No	recurrent or not	No	No	Dedicated and embedded schemes	Dedicated and embedded schemes	Private Sector and Insurances	No
Scope	National	Yes	No	Yes	Yes	Yes	Yes	Yes	Yes
	Subnational	Partial	No	Yes (annual average)	No	Yes	Yes	Yes	No
	Municipalities	No	No	No	No	No	No	No	No
	Years	1999-2014	2011	2009	1962-2014	2005 and 2012	2005 and 2012	Annual average of 2000 - 2005	fiscal years 2004 through 2018
Sources	Interviews	No	No	Yes	No	Yes	Yes	Yes	No
	Public Reports/budgets	Yes	Yes	Yes	Yes	Yes	Yes	Yes	Yes
	Survey	No	No	Yes	No	No	No	No	No

Source: Authors

In the following a more detailed overview of the national disaster risk management expenditure reviews that have been conducted in Japan, Australia, Switzerland, France, Austria, Colombia and Mexico is provided, before an overall assessment, conclusions and policy recommendations are discussed.

Japan

With the White Paper on Disaster Management, the Japanese Government set out to regularly assess on an annual basis the development of its disaster related expenditure at central government level, tracing back expenditure to as early as the 1960's and continuously reporting it in the White Paper. Disaster risk management related expenditures are distinguished into science and technology research, disaster prevention, land conservation (disaster management), and disaster reconstruction.

Figure 3.2 shows these annual levels expenditure since 1980. It illustrates that expenditure engaged in the aftermath of disasters changes depending on the occurrence and severity of disasters, with significant spikes in spending caused by large scale disasters. In addition, a comparison of disaster risk management spending against overall central-level budget shows that disaster risk management expenditure has been relatively volatile in the last decades; declining from an overall high in 1994/1995 (around 10 percent of general fund budget), when Kobe was hit by a 7.3 magnitude earthquake, to an all-time low in 2010 (at less than 2 percent), when the Japanese economy was in recession, to almost 6 percent in the aftermath of the Great East Japan Earthquake in 2011 (Figure 3.3).

Figure 3.2. Disaster prevention and reconstruction expenditure in Japan, 1980-2016

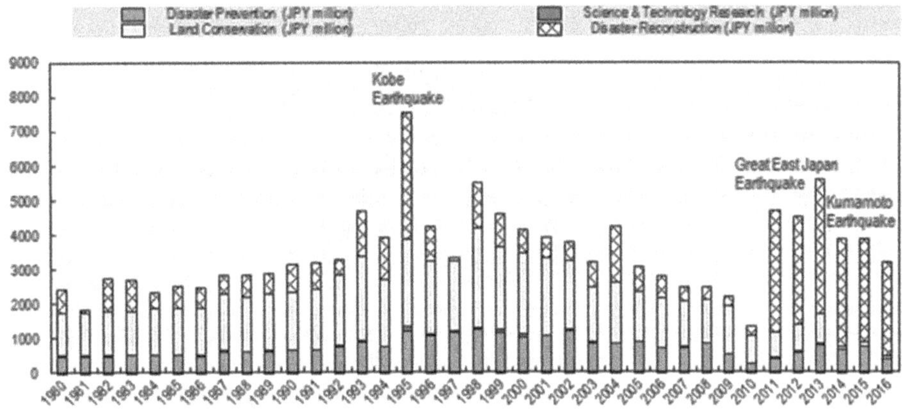

Note: In 2004 expenditure recording methods changed slightly making the comparison between budget estimates prior and after these changes less imprecise. The figures for the 2016 fiscal year are preliminary figures reflecting the initial budget.

Source: Cabinet Office Japan (2016)

Figure 3.3. Trends in central government disaster management expenditure in Japan

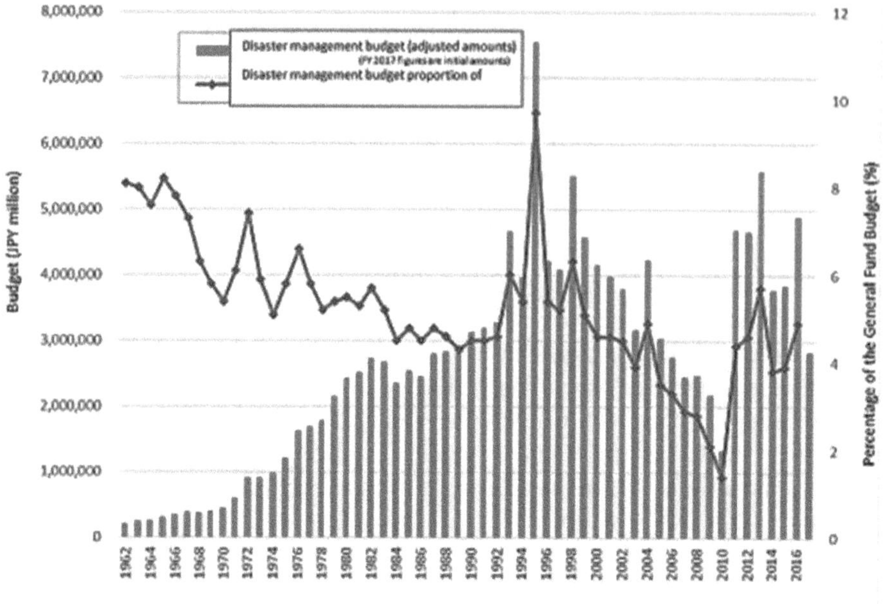

Disaster management budget (adjusted amounts)
(FY2017 figures are initial amounts)
Disaster management budget proportion of
Budget (JPY million)
Percentage of the General Fund Budget (%)

Source: Cabinet Office Japan (2017)

In Japan, subnational governments play an important role in financing post-disaster relief and recovery efforts, as well as disaster risk reduction measures. Data on sub-national expenditures are collected separately from the tracking of central government spending and featured in the White Paper on Local Public Finance. Based on the information gathered, Japan is able to demonstrate that although subnational governments provided substantial funding in support of recovery and reconstruction (Figure 3.4), the central government provides the majority of funding (Figure 3.5).

Figure 3.4. Subnational governments' post-disaster recovery and reconstruction expenditure for infrastructure, 2004-2015

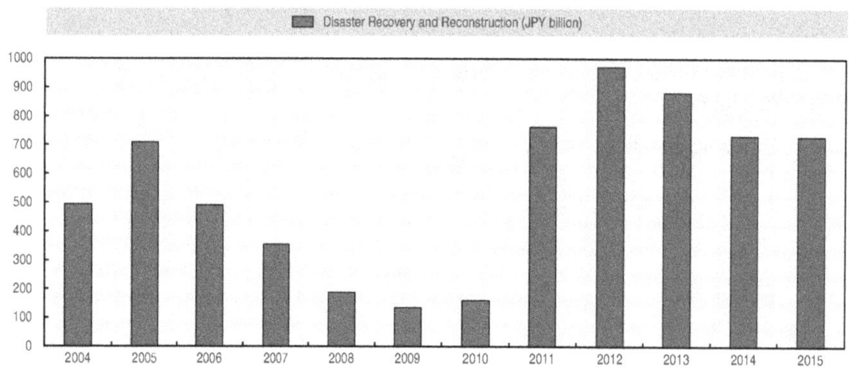

Source: based on Ministry of Internal Affairs and Communications (MIC) Japan (2016)

Figure 3.5. Financial resources of subnational governments' post-disaster recovery/reconstruction revenue for infrastructure in Japan, 2015

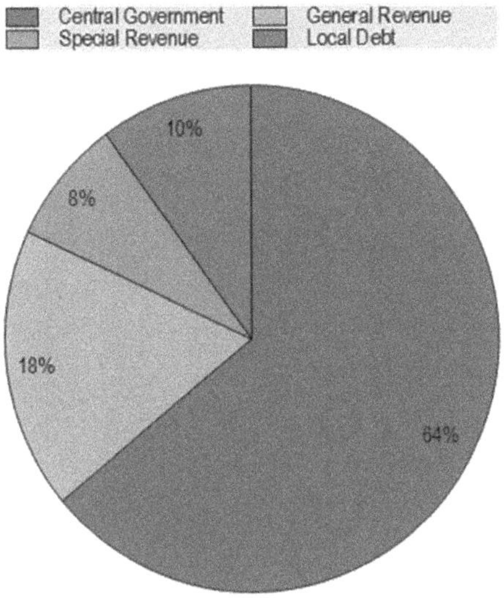

Source: based on Ministry of Internal Affairs and Communications (MIC) Japan (2016)

Australia

In Australia, the Council of Australian Governments, in co-operation with Australia's Bureau of Transport and Regional Economics (BTRE), collected and analysed government expenditure data related to disaster risk management at the Commonwealth and State/Territory levels for the 1999-2000 fiscal year (BTRE, 2001). The Australian Productivity Commission[3] has since continued this review. The expenditure data tracked by the Productivity Commission differentiates between pre-disaster and post-disaster event expenditure, as well as between expenditure spent on mitigation measures, disaster response and disaster relief and recovery.

The records show that central government spending on ex-ante disaster risk management (i.e. preparedness and risk prevention) has summed up to AUS$ 550 million (USD 415 million) between 2002 and 2014. In the same period the central government spent AUS$ 13 billion (USD 9.8 billion) on ex-post disaster risk management, with post-disaster recovery spending via the Natural Disaster Relief and Recovery Arrangements (NDRRA) accounting for the bulk of the funding. Figure 3.6 shows the development of annual central government expenditure for disaster risk management between 2002 and 2014.

Figure 3.6. Estimated disaster risk management expenditure in Australia in Mio AUS$, 2002/03 – 2014/15

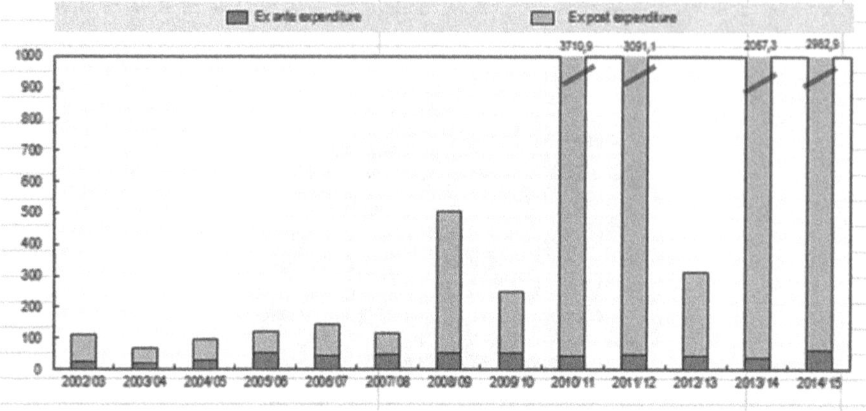

Source: based on Productivity Commission, 2014

The records illustrate that central government shares the responsibilities for disaster risk management with sub-national governments via the National Partnership Agreement on Natural Disaster Resilience (NPANDR). Through it, the central government spent AUS$ 115 million (USD 90 million) between 2009/10 and 2012/13, while sub-national governments added nearly the same amount (AUS$ 110 million; USD 88 million). Additional ex-ante spending comes from various central government programmes set-up to fund volunteer support, education and research, as well as from embedded spending at sub-national level, such as investments in infrastructure that is required to be built in a resilient way from the start. Spending under these programmes is however not reflected in the review conducted by the Australian Productivity Commission, as consistent time series data are unavailable.

Similarly, responsibilities for funding ex-post disaster risk management are shared across levels of government. The NDRRA and the Australian Government Disaster Recovery Payments (AGDRP) are the primary programmes for providing post-disaster recovery expenditure. Data on post-disaster spending outside these two cost-sharing arrangements is not reflected in the expenditure records tracked by the Productivity Commission, which suggests that tracking expenditure at sub-national government level is a complex endeavour.

Figure 3.7. Ex-ante versus ex-post disaster risk management expenditures at national level, Australia 2002-2014

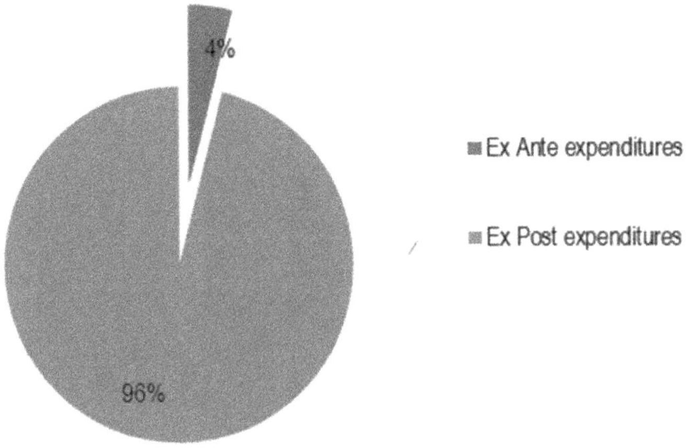

4%
96%
Ex Ante expenditures
Ex Post expenditures

Source: based on Productivity Commission, 2014

Switzerland

In the absence of a systematic and regular overview of the total budget allocation for disaster risk management in Switzerland, the Swiss National Platform for Natural Hazards (PLANAT) conducted a study in 2007 where it collected different expenditure figures from across levels of government, as well as from non-governmental actors. This study differentiated between expenditure spent on the management of each type of natural hazards (floods, avalanches, landslides, earthquakes, storms and extreme temperatures) in Switzerland. Publicly available databases on government expenditures and around 80 interviews constituted the basis for these estimates (PLANAT, 2014).

Unlike other expenditure frameworks, the review also assessed disaster risk management expenditure by private enterprises and households as well as public-private infrastructure operators through surveys and the consultations of experts. The study found that the insurance sector, private companies and households provided CHF 1.7 billion of the total CHF 2.9 billion. The review cautioned against the precision of its estimates as many data gaps called for extrapolations and assumptions to arrive at the total sum for each institution, hazard type and disaster risk management phase. National estimates could vary from +10 to –5 percent, subnational from + 20 to –10 percent. The highest degree of imprecision is expected for private sector estimates, potentially varying from +30 to -15 percent.

For 2015, PLANAT conducted a second survey of the public funding across levels of government for disaster risk prevention management. It found that, of the total annual amount for risk management, CHF 1.3 billion was spent on prevention, CHF 392 million on emergency interventions and CHF 1.1 billion on rehabilitation. Figures 3.8 and 3.9 show the evolution of national-level expenditures for floods and other natural hazards.

Figure 3.8. Expenditure for flood risk management at national level, 1972-2014

Source: Data submitted to authors by the Federal Statistical Office (2016)

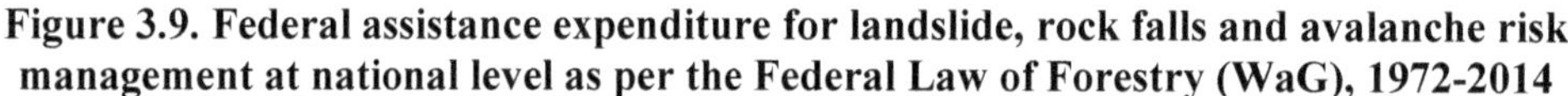

Figure 3.9. Federal assistance expenditure for landslide, rock falls and avalanche risk management at national level as per the Federal Law of Forestry (WaG), 1972-2014

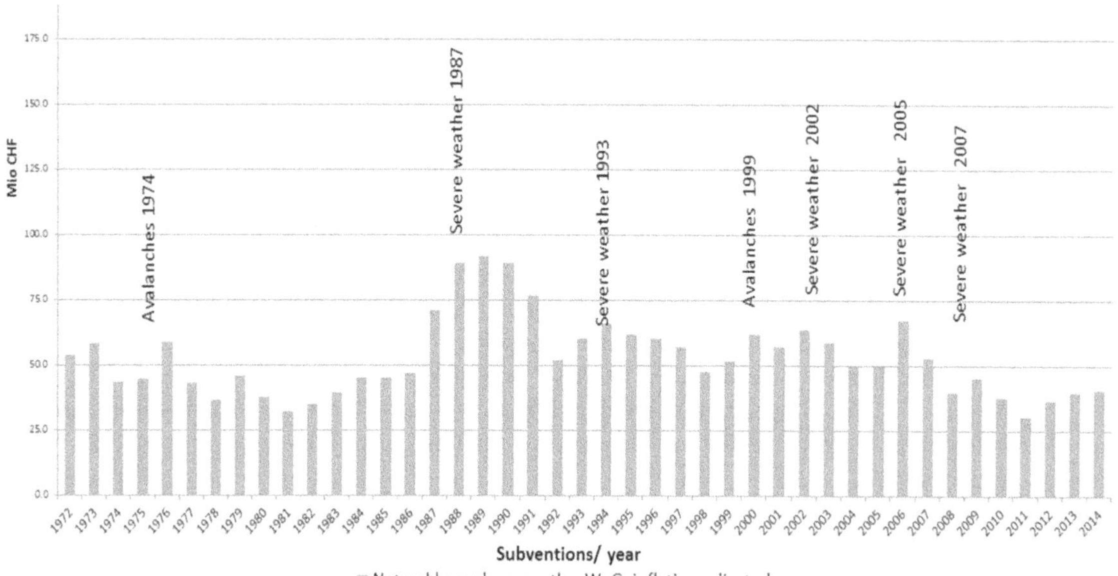

Source: Data submitted to authors by the Federal Statistical Office (2016)

France

The French General Commission for Sustainable Development (*Commissariat Général au Développement Durable*) within the Ministry of Ecology, Sustainable Development and Energy conducted a public expenditure analysis in 2009 focusing on ex-ante disaster risk management expenditure[4], which is comparable to the Swiss approach. Other, ex-post related expenditure such as response or rehabilitation was not included in the review. A focus on natural hazards (floods, forest fires, atmospheric disasters, avalanches, earthquakes, volcanic eruptions and landslides) was chosen, excluding other, man-made threats. The evaluation of expenditures by the national government is based on the analysis of budget reports and yearly performance evaluations of individual programmes.

Estimates for disaster risk management expenditure on the subnational level are derived from projects and programmes financed by national funds as well as individual interviews with stakeholders in local municipalities (with a population larger than 100,000), local basin organisations and other relevant stakeholders. All stakeholders had to indicate the origin of revenue flows in order to avoid double-counting. The estimated sum for subnational disaster risk management spending in 2009 is likely an underestimation as programmes, as ex-ante disaster risk management spending and expenditure by small municipalities were not counted. Expenditure items are assigned to hazard categories (Table 3.3), to functions (by ministry), or programmes and actions. Disaster risk management spending by public operators could not be tracked with the exception of public water agencies which invested EUR 5.3 million in prevention and mitigation of floods. In 2009, the French national government spent EUR 340 million for ex-ante disaster risk management, of which flood-related expenditures accounted for nearly half of all disaster risk management spending. Most sources of funding for disaster risk management expenditure items were financed by the Barnier Fund[5].

Table 3.3. National government DRM expenditure in 2009 by hazard type

Hazards	Expenditures by national government (in EUR million)	% of total expenditure
Floods	155	46
Earthquakes	62	18
Forest Fires	41	12
Avalanches	5	1
Multi-risks	77	23

Source: Nicklaus, D., Chaillou, D., Crespin, N. and Peinturier C. (2013)

The estimated expenditure on the subnational level entails a high degree of imprecision as it derives from the calculated annual average of all projects in subnational governments, which are financed by national funds. All projects by subnational governments that received national government funding were analysed and an average spending estimate for 2009 was counted for each programme. This amounted to around EUR 230 to 244 million. Expenditures at the subnational level could not be categorised into hazard categories as in the case of national DRM spending.

Finally the review included funding received from the European Union (EU)[6] for disaster risk prevention and mitigation. The annual funding received from the EU amount to an estimated EUR 21 million to co-finance prevention and mitigation of central and sub-national government-assisted projects. Counting all of the items together, an annual total of around EUR 596 to 610 million in public expenditure was estimated for ex-ante disaster risk management spending in France. As mentioned earlier, this is likely to be an underestimation due to limited data from public infrastructure operators and local governments (Table 3.4).

Table 3.4. Public DRM expenditure in 2009 by government institutions

Actor or category	Expenditures (in EUR million)
National Government (including Barnier Fund)	340
State owned critical operators (except water operator)	Non-estimated
Water operator	5
Sub-national governments	230-244
Regions	56-58
Departments	108-110
Municipalities	66-76
European Union	21
Total	596-610

Source: Nicklaus, D., Chaillou, D., Crespin, N. and Peinturier C. (2013)

Austria

In Austria, the Federal Ministry of Agriculture, Forestry, Environment and Water Management (BMLFUW) has been collecting expenditure data regarding natural hazards management from the three main authorities responsible for disaster risk management: the Austrian Service for Torrent and Avalanche Control (WLV), the Federal Water Engineering Administration (BWV), and the Federal Ministry of Transport, Innovation and Technology Management (BMVIT). While the available data is relatively comprehensive, it is not fully publicly accessible, nor exhaustive, as the substantial subnational contributions throughout the disaster risk management cycle are for instance not reflected. The records show that at central level, on average EUR 250 million per year are spent for prevention and mitigation measures against flood and Alpine hazards by these three agencies (Figure 3.10) (OECD, *forthcoming*).

Figure 3.10. Annual federal disaster risk prevention and mitigation expenditure from 2002-2014 (in 2010 prices)

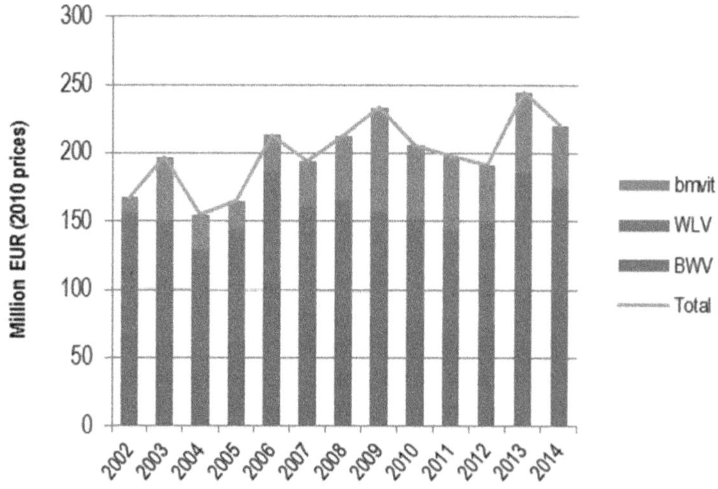

Source: OECD 2015 in-country mission meetings; OECD, *forthcoming*

Looking at the allocation of prevention spending across Austria, Figure 3.11 shows the expenditure by the two different disaster risk prevention services within provinces. The majority of expenditure by the WLV is concentrated in mountainous provinces, such as Tyrol, Salzburg and Styria. Whereas the largest part of BWV spending is undertaken in low-lying provinces with large rivers, such as Lower Austria.

Figure 3.11. Federal disaster risk prevention and mitigation expenditure by province in 2014 (in Mio EUR)

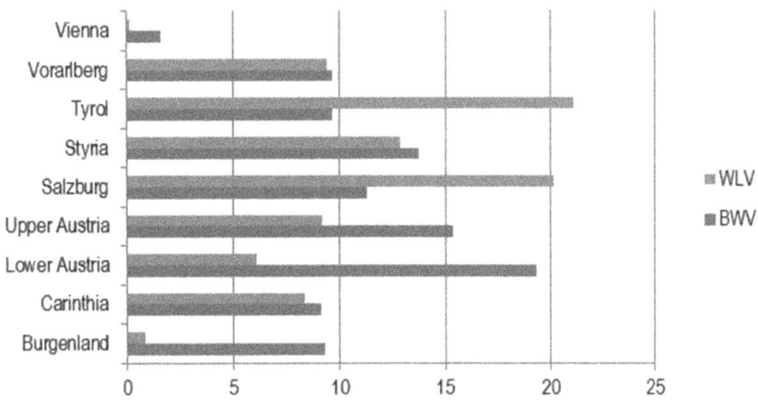

Source: OECD 2015 in-country mission meetings

Colombia and Mexico

As part of a larger analytical work the World Bank conducted an expenditure study for disaster risk management based on the assessment of a number of country cases including Columbia and Mexico (de la Fuente, 2010). The study aimed at tracking expenditures over the time period 1998 to 2008. This study collected disaster risk management expenditure items according to phases of the DRM cycle rather than according to ministerial or departmental functions. This allowed for obtaining a rough estimate of ex-ante and ex-post disaster spending in a country, but without capturing other characteristics such as for example whether they are recurring budgetary items, what type of costs (capital investments or other), or recipient department.

Within each hazard category each expenditure item is either classified into ex-ante disaster expenditure, such as preparedness, risk identification, mitigation and transfer or into an ex-post disaster expenditure category such as emergency response, rehabilitation and reconstruction efforts. The classifications on disaster risk management entail expenditures pertaining to measures of vulnerability reduction such as structural measures as well as land-use planning and building codes and social programs to promote risk awareness and set incentives for implementing mitigation measures. Disaster risk management expenditure also included costs for risk mapping and hazard assessments as well as training and research. Disaster risk transfer expenditures such as insurance premiums for earthquake or crop insurances are also taken into account for the expenditure framework. In Mexico earthquake insurance expenditures accrued to over 70 percent of total ex-ante disaster expenditures during the investigated time period. However the framework does not cover expenditures made for capital investments that are only indirectly contributing to disaster risk management and that are not labelled as a disaster risk management budget item. Moreover, disaster risk management expenditure disbursed at sub-national level are not collected. The results of this expenditure framework indicate that ex-post disaster spending may exceed ex-ante disaster expenditures in Mexico, but not in Colombia (Figure 3.12 and Table 3.5). Nonetheless, ex-ante spending has increased gradually suggesting an increasing importance of proactive disaster spending over the years.

Figure 3.12. Public ex-ante and ex-post DRM expenditure, 1998-2008 (in million USD, 2008 prices)

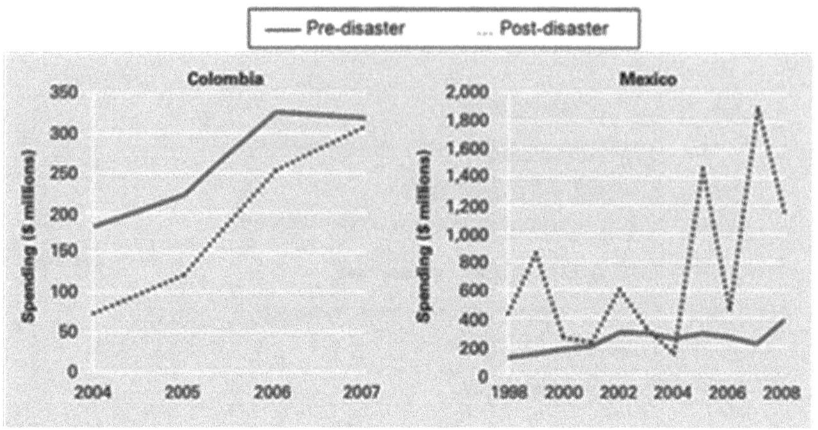

Source: de la Fuente (2010)

Table 3.5. Accumulated ex-ante and ex-post disaster expenditure during 1998- 2008

	Total (in USD million, 2008 prices)	Pre- to Post-expenditure ratio
Columbia	1,807.52	1.38 (Pre: 58% and Post: 42%)
Mexico	10,403.45	0.34 (Pre: 25% and Post: 75%)

Source: de la Fuente (2010)

United States of America

In the United States, the Department of Homeland Security (DHS) creates annual budget overviews that outline the budget of the Federal Emergency Management Agency (FEMA) among other remits. The DHS' website lists all budget documents from fiscal years 2004 through 2018.

The annually published budget of the DHS provides a comprehensive overview over FEMA expenditure, disaggregated spending information (Figure 3.13). The data shows that overall FEMA budgets have been relatively stable over the past five years, with few budgetary variations. In addition, in 2013 the DHS published the Federal Program Inventory to facilitate stakeholder understanding of federal programs and facilitate coordination across government. The inventory provides a snapshot over all federal programmes under DHS jurisdiction. Among other budget items, this expenditure overview illustrates aggregate federal spending throughout the disaster risk management cycle as carried out by FEMA between 2012 and 2014 (Department of Homeland Security, 2017a; Department of Homeland Security, 2017b).

Figure 3.13. Annual budgets of the United States Federal Emergency Management Agency, 2012-2016 (in thousand USD)

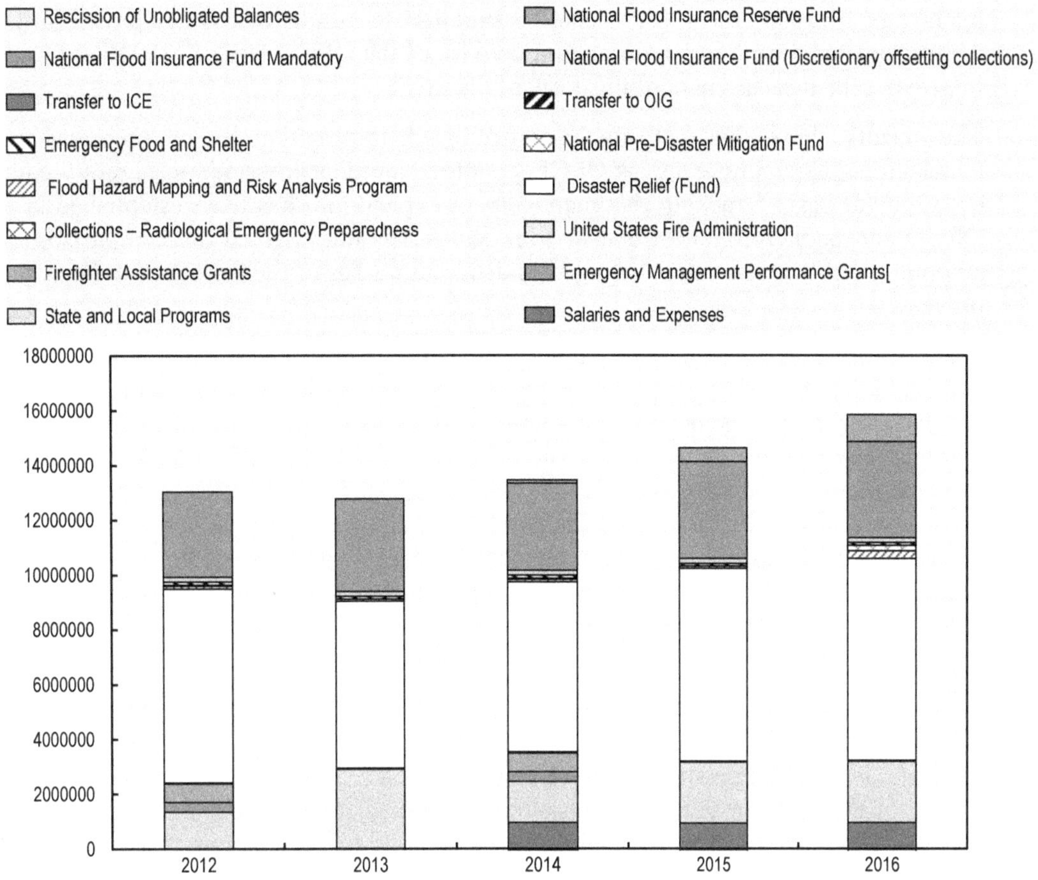

Source: Department of Homeland Security (2017a)

In addition, the DHS' performance and financial reports provide information that enables an assessment of the effectiveness of the performance and stewardship of resources by both decision makers and the general public. These reports present detailed expenditure data and an overview over the various agencies' work to implement the respective agency's annual objectives.

The federal DHS/FEMA does however also illustrate the complexity inherent to disaster risk management expenditure overviews, as for example the classification of spending into budget items has changed throughout the years and as not all disaster risk management spending features in it. Sub-national spending, for instance, is not reflected, but nonetheless accounts for a significant part of overall expenditure in support of disaster risk management. Similarly, embedded spending is not specifically listed in the annual budgets, as this would feature in the respective budgets of the agency that carries out that project. To arrive at an exhaustive snapshot of all public spending in support of disaster risk management, the existing information regarding FEMA's budget would need to be systematically expanded with all sub-national disaster risk management budget data and embedded expenditure information from other central and sub-national budgets.

3.4. Discussion of results

This chapter has summarised the rationale behind collecting information on disaster risk management expenditures. It presented a summary of results of country level efforts that were identified during the multi-annual activity of the OECD High Level Risk Forum on improving the measurement of the costs of disasters.

The results show that not much consolidated information exists on disaster risk management expenditure across OECD countries and that information is rarely gathered on a regular basis. Tracking risk management expenditure has been established in some OECD and partner countries and in some cases this has enabled the comparison of the amount of public expenditure engaged in different phases of the disaster risk management process.

A number of challenges that make tracking expenditure difficult persist. In the absence of dedicated disaster risk management budget lines, one challenge is to identify expenditure on disaster risk management across sectors and levels of government. Depending on the administrative set-up of a country this exercise may be highly complex and requires research. Another challenge entails identifying "embedded" spending items, i.e. spending on a project that only partly contributes to risk management such as the meteorological office whose forecasting is a crucial element for early warning systems. The collection of such information is rarely mandatory, which makes it difficult for risk managers to extract such information across ministries and municipalities, as it has an administrative cost.

There are a number of OECD countries that can demonstrate the significant value of collecting loss and expenditure statistics systematically to inform policy making. For example, in Japan these statistics have enabled flood risk managers to show that over the course of the past ten years their risk reduction investments have significantly reduced loss of lives from flooding. Japan has also been able to demonstrate that total economic losses can be reduced due to investment in ex-ante flood risk reduction measures, although increases in asset concentration in flood areas remains a challenge.

Notes

[1] The online OECD survey was filled out by 17 countries (Australia, Austria, Canada, Colombia, Costa Rica, Denmark, Estonia, Finland, France, Japan, Israel, Mexico, Norway, Poland, Slovak Republic, Sweden, and Turkey). Annex B provides the full list of names of the responding institution in each country as well as the survey.

[2] More information on the workshops and presentation material can be found under the following links: www.oecd.org/gov/risk/joint-expert-meeting-on-disaster-loss-data.htm

[3] The Productivity Commission is the Australian Government's independent research and advisory body on a range of economic, social and environmental issues affecting the welfare of Australians.

[4] Ex-ante DRM spending includes: research, surveillance, communication, mitigation, crisis preparation, case studies after disasters.

[5] www.eure.gouv.fr/Politiques-publiques/Securite-et-protection-de-la-population/Risques-naturels-et-technologiques-Nuisances/Risques-naturels/Complement-risques-naturels-et-technologiques/Fonds-de-prevention-des-risques-naturels-majeurs-Fonds-Barnier

[6] This concerns the European Regional Development Fund (ERDF) and the European Agricultural Fund for Rural Development (EAFRD).

References

Cabinet Office Japan (2016). White Paper Disaster Management in Japan 2016, www.bousai.go.jp/kyoiku/panf/pdf/WP2016_DM_Full_Version.pdf

Cabinet Office Japan (2017). White Paper Disaster Management in Japan 2017, www.bousai.go.jp/kyoiku/panf/pdf/WP2017_DM_Full_Version.pdf

De la Fuente, A. (2010). Government Expenditures in Pre and Post Disaster Risk Management, Background Note for World Bank–U.N. Assessment on the Economics of Disaster Risk Reduction. Natural Hazards, Unnatural Disasters: The Economics of Effective Prevention; www.gfdrr.org/sites/gfdrr/files/Country%20Disaster%20Expenditures%20Note.pdf

Department of Homeland Security (2017a). DHS Budget, www.dhs.gov/dhs-budget

Department of Homeland Security (2017b). FY 2016 Agency Financial Report, www.dhs.gov/sites/default/files/publications/dhs_agency_financial_report_fy2016.pdf

Gamper, C., Singer, B., Alton, L. and M. Petrie (2017). Managing disaster-related contingent liabilities in public finance frameworks, OECD Publishing, Paris, http://dx.doi.org/10.1787/a6e0265a-en

Ministry of Internal Affairs and Communications (MIC) Japan (2016), White Paper on Local Public Finance, 2016/2017, www.soumu.go.jp/iken/zaisei/28data/chihouzaisei_2016_en.pdf

Nicklaus, D., Chaillou, D., Crespin, N. and C. Peinturier (2013). Les dépenses publiques et les bénéfices de la prévention des risques naturels. [Public expenditure and beneficiaries of disaster risk prevention], Studies & Documents n.97, September 2013. Commissariat Général au Développement Durable, http://temis.documentation.developpement-durable.gouv.fr/docs/Temis/0079/Temis-0079105/20910.pdf

OECD (2014), Recommendation on the Governance of Critical Risks, www.oecd.org/gov/risk/recommendation-on-governance-of-critical-risks.htm

OECD (2017), Boosting Disaster Prevention through Innovative Risk Governance: Insights from Austria, France and Switzerland, OECD Reviews of Risk Management Policies, OECD Publishing, Paris, http://dx.doi.org/10.1787/9789264281370-en.

PLANAT (2007). Strategie Naturgefahren Schweiz. Umsetzung des Aktionsplans PLANAT 2005-2008. Jährliche Aufwendungen für den Schutz vor Naturgefahren in der Schweiz [Natural Hazards Strategy Switzerland. Implementation of the PLANAT 2005-2008 Action Plan. Annual Expenditure for the Protection against Natural Hazards in Switzerland]. National Platform for Natural Hazards, Switzerland

PLANAT (2014). Security Level for Natural Hazards: Strategy Protection against Natural Hazards, National Platform for Natural Hazards, Biel, www.planat.ch/fileadmin/PLANAT/planat_pdf/alle_2012/2011-2015/PLANAT_2014__Security_Level_for_Natural_Hazards.pdf

Productivity Commission (2014). Natural Disaster Funding Arrangements, Inquiry Report No. 74, Canberra. Volume 1&2, http://www.pc.gov.au/inquiries/completed/disaster-funding/report/disaster-funding-volume1.pdf; http://www.pc.gov.au/inquiries/completed/disaster-funding/report/disaster-funding-volume2.pdf

World Bank and Global Facility for Disaster Reduction and Recovery (GFDRR) (2012). Analysis of Disaster Risk Management in Colombia A Contribution to the Creation of Public Policies, www.gfdrr.org/sites/gfdrr/files/publication/Analysis_of_Disaster_Risk_Management_in_Colombia.pdf

4. Summary and next steps

This chapter revisits the objectives behind improving the evidence base or the measurement of the costs of disasters. It provides an overview of the main policy relevant findings that can be drawn from the research underpinning this report. In the outlook section steps are proposed to continue enhancing national as well as international efforts to collect data on the cost of disasters.

4.1. Revisiting the rationale

Critical risks continue to pose a range of negative impacts on OECD societies and economies. Water-related disasters such as floods are among the most frequently occurring ones across OECD countries. The increases in economic damages are estimated to have outpaced national investments in disaster risk reduction. However, this claim is more intuitive than supported by data driven analysis. Indeed there is limited comparable data available on the costs of disasters, in terms of national expenditure to manage disaster risks or information on ex-post recorded disaster losses and damages, which are generally considered to be incomplete and underestimated.

It has been recognised that standardised and comparable information on expenditure for disaster risk management and disaster losses and damages help countries' governments, and non-governmental risk management stakeholders alike, to evaluate the benefits of their disaster risk investments. From an international perspective, such data brings significant value in the form of comprehensive indicators on global disaster risk reduction objectives as envisaged in the Sustainable Development Goals Agenda as well as the Sendai Framework for Disaster Risk Reduction.

This report presented the results of a multi-year activity conducted by the OECD High Level Risk Forum to document countries' current engagement in assessing the costs of disasters. The objective of the work was to take account of ongoing national as well as international efforts that record ex-post economic losses stemming from disasters as well as contribute to the far less developed expenditure aspects of the costs of disasters. The latter part of the work sought to assess ongoing national initiatives to systematically collect information on disaster risk management expenditures with a view to provide policy makers with information that allows them to track more systematically how much they spend and for how much of the disaster costs they are liable for, as well as whether their spending efforts actually lead to future reductions in negative impacts suffered from disasters.

Chapter 1 provides an introduction into the main concepts of the costs of disasters, notably disaster related losses and damages on the one hand and public expenditures to manage disasters on the other. The introductory discussion highlights the expected benefits of addressing this topic on an international level, in terms of the comparability and standardisation of data collection efforts, but also the usefulness of improving the measurement basis across countries so as to better address the transboundary characteristics of critical risks OECD member and partner countries are confronted with. The chapter therefore also highlighted the ongoing international efforts to improve countries' evidence base on the costs of disasters as well as the contribution of OECD countries in that discussion.

Chapter 2 summarises the results of a stock-taking exercise that included an assessment of the comparability of existing country loss data sets in international disaster losses and damage databases on the one hand, and a more detailed progress report and comparison of country-level data in OECD and some of its partner countries, which relies on responses to a dedicated OECD survey. The results presented in the chapter also reflect the outcomes of discussions and additional information shared by countries during two expert meetings that were held on loss data collection at the OECD in 2014 and 2016. The chapter highlights the considerable efforts that some countries' governmental as well as non-governmental actors have put into gathering existing information on disaster damages and losses ex-post of disaster events. Based on the information presented, the chapter draws out the persisting shortcomings in terms of comprehensiveness and comparability of current country-level efforts.

Chapter 3 turns the report's focus to disaster risk management expenditure, which is the considerably less studied part of the measurement cost discussion. It brings together the findings of an extensive desk research, complemented by OECD survey questions as well as country discussions held during the two expert meetings. The chapter highlights the value of improved information on disaster risk expenditure to inform policy makers about the effectiveness of their resource allocation for reducing disaster impacts over time. It does so by illustrating good country practices to gather such information in dedicated expenditure reviews. Given the sporadic nature of countries conducting disaster risk management expenditure reviews, the chapter seeks to discuss the existing challenges to gather this information and recommends solutions for countries to address present shortcomings.

4.2. Summary of the main findings

Several international disaster statistics repositories exist that are working to improve the quality of disaster information and to increase its comparability across countries. As information on disaster impacts is not consistently recorded by national governments, so are statistics reported in a standard manner in international databases.

Economic loss data is collected by many countries, but information is not always centralised in one national database. Different institutions, from national to municipal level, are active in the collection of data for economic losses from disasters. More than two thirds of respondent countries have a systematic process for economic loss data collection, but only half of them store this information in an official centralised repository. This might be the result of countries' lack of a lead institution that coordinates part of the efforts in gathering economic losses.

The information on economic losses remains difficult to compare. Although definitions exist for calculating direct physical impacts, such as damaged buildings, agricultural assets and civil infrastructure, this is not consistently done for all disaster events across countries. Other losses are even less reported. These include losses associated with the interruption of activities at business and household levels, transport interruption or interruption of other lifeline infrastructure. More intangible costs such as the impact on health or the environment are hardly ever evaluated. Economic losses are only reported for 30-40% of disaster events in OECD countries, and for those events where numbers exist, they can vary widely from one data repository to another.

On the disaster risk management expenditure side, the review work showed that only few OECD and partner countries have attempted to systematically take account of and understand their disaster risk management expenditures. In countries, where disaster risk management expenditure is tracked, this information collection effort is not regularly carried out. Instead, the expenditure information that exists at the national level is usually the result of a specific project or programme that was implemented to retrieve expenditure information from sectoral budgets across relevant sectors and across different levels of government. The reason for this is that disaster risk management does often not exist as an expenditure category as such in public accounts, but is "embedded" in other expenditure categories.

The collected information confirms that there is room for improving the collection and standardisation of data on disaster risk management expenditures across OECD countries.

Such information can be obtained from governments in a comparative way and on a continuous basis.

Guidelines and international standards for losses and damage as well as for expenditure accounting for disaster risk management need improvement. The difference between direct and indirect economic losses remains ill-established.

Going forward

This report provided a snapshot of country efforts as they are continuously evolving, take time to establish and are undergoing considerable policy changes at the time of being reviewed. The country data reviews conducted for this report show that data collection processes of this kind take time to mature. The reviews clearly demonstrate that existing records on disaster losses and damages have evolved significantly in terms of frequency and also breath in the information that has been reported over the past decade compared preceding ones. In addition, countries report important ongoing national policy reforms that they expect to strengthen their data repositories in the near future, which has been partly prompted by international efforts, such as the Sendai process as well as the Sustainable Development Goals agenda that both aim at improving countries' systematic and comprehensive measurement of the costs of disasters in the future. In light of this, the results discussed in this report should be viewed as a snapshot of a continuous improvement process that is undergoing many changes and that would merit a re-assessment in some years.

As this fact gathering process by the OECD High Level Risk Forum, and other ongoing similar activities have shown, there is value in establishing and nurturing a community of country experts on progress in the measurement of the costs of disasters to inform and inspire countries' subsequent steps in their work by fostering country exchanges among practitioners and experts alike. There are notable ongoing regional initiatives that bring together practitioners across countries, such as the Asia-Pacific Expert Group Meeting on Disaster-related Statistics, or the EU's Joint Research Centre's bi-annual Loss Data Working Group Meetings. OECD countries have a unique value to contribute in these discussions, as they benefit from widely and well established statistical processes and institutions that readily provide the technical capacity for developing and improving disaster related statistics. The outcomes of discussions of progress among OECD members could continue to inform the post-Sendai implementation reporting process as well as the monitoring of the implementation of the Sustainable Development Goals.

Given its position and expertise there is an opportunity for the OECD to inform the improvement of the standards developed for disaster loss and expenditure data collection. Advancements have been made to defining social losses by academia and stakeholders at national and international level in charge of collecting this type of data. In complement to this the OECD would be well placed to contribute to improvements of direct and indirect economic loss assessments as well as expenditure reporting standards that increase comparability within and across countries.

Annex A. Improving the Evidence Base on the Costs of Disasters: OECD Expert Meeting Summaries

1st Expert Meeting held on November 21 2014: Summary Points

Objectives of the meeting

The overall goal of the meeting was to contribute to improving countries' disaster risk management policies as set out in the *OECD Recommendation of the Council on the Governance of Critical Risks*. With the development of a framework for assessing disaster risk-related costs the OECD seeks to improve the evidence base for evaluating and comparing risk management policies. The goal of the workshop was to discuss the state of the art of national engagements to collect information on disaster losses and to propose and discuss a framework for public expenditure on disaster risk management, exploring the possibilities to mainstream the initial pilot framework.

The objectives of the meeting were to:

- better understand current country practices to consolidate expenditure data on disaster risk management ex-ante and ex-post;
- distil good practices and existing challenges when it comes to consolidating public expenditure data for disaster risk management, and
- facilitate exchange and contribute to the discussion on how governments can introduce methodologies and standards to produce comparative data on disaster risk expenditures to inform policy decisions.

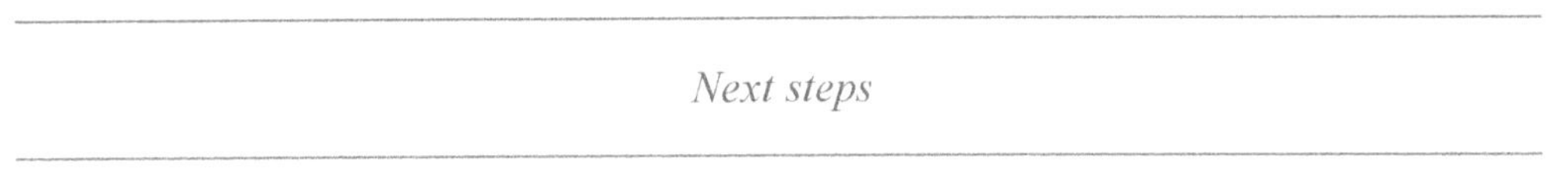

Next steps

It is recommended for the OECD to contribute to setting a common standard on defining economic losses to increase availability and comparability of data. International and private sector efforts that collect comparable disaster statistics would welcome if the OECD engaged in establishing guidance and references on the calculation of direct and indirect economic losses. This would provide meta-data providers with a tool to guide country data collection processes, and would help inform countries directly on how they could improve their disaster information collection procedures. This could also contribute to the efforts of the global risk management community to learn of and adopt a new standard of collecting economic loss information, and could inform experts' discussions during the meetings in Sendai in March 2015 to discuss the follow-up of the Hyogo Framework for Action (HFA). These meetings will seek input on the indicators to be used to evaluate the performance of the next HFA. The reference work of the European Union and the Centre for Epidemiology (CRED) may underline the value of the OECD as a possible reference point in their consultation processes.

The development of a common framework for accounting risk management expenditure is a novel approach that would bring significant value to risk managers in countries. As such the approach is highly welcomed but will require further efforts over the coming year. The fact that little work has been done on this internationally is a key advantage as it allows the OECD to start with a new definition, rather than having to reconcile existing approaches.

In going forward a phased approach is needed. It is suggested to:

- Propose a framework that is simple, aggregate and robust enough for countries to provide information, and yet accurate and informative enough for policy making (i.e. it should enable to distinguish ex-ante and ex-post spending).
- Focus on a few hazards at first so as to be able to compare across countries. An all-hazards approach to expenditure might be difficult to achieve across OECD countries at first. It is suggested for countries to report expenditure data according to their most important risks.
- Collect data on a voluntary basis, starting with countries that have already engaged in such an effort. This should also help refine the definition of common reporting standards.
- Collect such expenditure information every 3-5 years, given administrative and institutional constraints in countries.

Summary of key discussion points

The workshop underlined the importance of disaster statistics for policy making. In Japan these statistics enable risk managers to show the effectiveness of their risk reduction measures for comparable disaster events. Over the course of 10 years, on average, these measures have shown to reduce asset loss as well as the loss of lives by 90%. Japan is able to demonstrate that total economic losses were significantly reduced with only a fraction of the expected losses invested in risk reduction measures. Some, but not all, OECD countries have a clear framework, set forth in DRM legal documents, on how to assess actual losses after disasters.

Several international disaster statistics repositories exist that are working to improve the quality of disaster information and to increase its comparability across countries. Information on disaster events is not consistently reported by national governments, nor are statistics reported in a standard manner in international databases. Although significant improvements have been made in the definition of a range of social indicators, e.g. the deaths associated with disasters, ambiguity persists in the definition of other social loss indicators, such as "missing people" or "affected people" that are still subject to relatively large ambiguities.

The information on actual economic losses remains difficult to compare. Although straightforward definitions exist for calculating direct physical impacts, such as affected buildings, agricultural assets and civil infrastructure, this is not consistently done for all disaster events across countries. Other losses are even less reported. These include indirect losses such as interruption of activities at business and household levels, transport interruption or interruption of lifelines or business activities. More intangible costs such as the impact on health or the environment are hardly ever accounted for due to difficulties in monetisation. As indirect and intangible losses are included to different extents, the comparability is not given. Economic losses are only reported for 30-40% of disaster events, and for those events where numbers exists, they can vary widely.

Gathering and comparing loss estimation methods of countries brings added value. The analyses of various damage estimation methods of countries and sharing them are useful exercises as this helps to design better estimation methods, with a clear focus to contribute to increasing the accuracy of existing disaster statistics. Coupled with actual loss assessment it is useful for countries to understand how they can conduct forward-looking ex-ante loss estimations, which can inform policy decisions especially on a project to project basis.

Collecting data on public (and private) expenditure for risk management is novel and could inform the assessment of the effectiveness of risk management policies. Systematic information on risk management expenditure, in combination with data on disaster losses would allow policy makers to evaluate whether risk management spending is effective in reducing the harmful impact of disasters. It would contribute to transparency and to promote risk management within countries. A common language to inform common approaches across countries in terms of risk management expenditure tracking would be valuable. The private sector would appreciate a method on risk expenditure as this would allow them to better assess the level of improvement in resilience against risks.

Tracking risk management expenditure has been established in a number of countries to promote a shift in investments from ex-post to ex-ante investments in risk reduction measures. The bulk of risk management funding still goes towards recovery and rehabilitation after disasters. Providing a full picture on where disaster spending flows helps to make the case for increased prevention and mitigation as well as preparedness funding. Additional motivators to collect such information were to ensure that level of investment is proportionate to risk, to ensure appropriate cost sharing arrangements, to demonstrate performance of risk management spending in reducing impacts in the long term.

However, expenditure information is not collected consistently. Very few countries systematically collect information on public (and private) expenditures. Australia, for example, collects this information regularly, but does so only for rehabilitation investments and not for overall risk management. In France, this has been done only for prevention investments. Physical infrastructure investments are widely included, but soft, non-structural investments in prevention are often not captured. The inclusion of private (e.g. HH and business) expenditure is more difficult – e.g. a questionnaire in France yielded little response. Analysing local budgets is important, but difficult to do without a proper mandate.

A common approach to accounting risk management expenditure is challenging. The countries that have collected such information have come across difficulties. In most countries there is no central repository (such as the national accounts) that clearly distinguishes and accounts for risk management. One challenge is therefore to identify all units that invest in risk management across sectors and levels of government. Depending on the administrative set-up of a country this exercise may be highly complex and requires research. Another challenge entails identifying "embedded" spending items, i.e. spending on a project that only partly contributes to risk management such as the meteorological office whose forecasting is a crucial element for early warning systems. The collection of such information is rarely mandatory, which makes it difficult for risk managers to extract such information across ministries and municipalities, as it has an administrative cost.

2nd Expert Meeting (jointly organised between the European Commission, the OECD and the Placard Project) held on 26-28 October 2016

Objectives of the meeting

The overall goal of the meeting was to contribute to improving countries' disaster risk management policies as set out in the *OECD Recommendation of the Council on the Governance of Critical Risks*. With the development of a framework for assessing disaster risk-related costs the OECD seeks to improve the evidence base for evaluating and comparing risk management policies. The goal of the workshop was to discuss the state of the art of national engagements to collect information on disaster losses and to propose and discuss a framework for public expenditure on disaster risk management, exploring the possibilities to mainstream the initial pilot framework.

The objectives of the meeting were to:

- better understand current country practices to consolidate expenditure data on disaster risk management ex-ante and ex-post;
- distil good practices and existing challenges when it comes to consolidating public expenditure data for disaster risk management, and
- facilitate exchange and contribute to the discussion on how governments can introduce methodologies and standards to produce comparative data on disaster risk expenditures to inform policy decisions.

Next steps

It is recommended for the OECD to contribute to setting a common standard on defining economic losses to increase availability and comparability of data. International and private sector efforts that collect comparable disaster statistics would welcome if the OECD engaged in establishing guidance and references on the calculation of direct and indirect economic losses. This would provide meta-data providers with a tool to guide country data collection processes, and would help inform countries directly on how they could improve their disaster information collection procedures. This could also contribute to the efforts of the global risk management community to learn of and adopt a new standard of collecting economic loss information, and could inform experts' discussions during the meetings in Sendai in March 2015 to discuss the follow-up of the Hyogo Framework for Action (HFA). These meetings will seek input on the indicators to be used to evaluate the performance of the next HFA. The reference work of the European Union and the Centre for Epidemiology (CRED) may underline the value of the OECD as a possible reference point in their consultation processes.

The development of a common framework for accounting risk management expenditure is a novel approach that would bring significant value to risk managers in countries. As such the approach is highly welcomed but will require further efforts over the coming year. The fact that little work has been done on this internationally is a key advantage as it allows the OECD to start with a new definition, rather than having to reconcile existing approaches.

In going forward a phased approach is needed. It is suggested to:

- Propose a framework that is simple, aggregate and robust enough for countries to provide information, and yet accurate and informative enough for policy making (i.e. it should enable to distinguish ex-ante and ex-post spending).
- Focus on a few hazards at first so as to be able to compare across countries. An all-hazards approach to expenditure might be difficult to achieve across OECD countries at first. It is suggested for countries to report expenditure data according to their most important risks.
- Collect data on a voluntary basis, starting with countries that have already engaged in such an effort. This should also help refine the definition of common reporting standards.
- Collect such expenditure information every 3-5 years, given administrative and institutional constraints in countries.

Summary of key discussion points

The workshop underlined the importance of disaster statistics for policy making. In Japan these statistics enable risk managers to show the effectiveness of their risk reduction measures for comparable disaster events. Over the course of 10 years, on average, these measures have shown to reduce asset loss as well as the loss of lives by 90%. Japan is able to demonstrate that total economic losses were significantly reduced with only a fraction of the expected losses invested in risk reduction measures. Some, but not all, OECD countries have a clear framework, set forth in DRM legal documents, on how to assess actual losses after disasters.

Several international disaster statistics repositories exist that are working to improve the quality of disaster information and to increase its comparability across countries. Information on disaster events is not consistently reported by national governments, nor are statistics reported in a standard manner in international databases. Although significant improvements have been made in the definition of a range of social indicators, e.g. the deaths associated with disasters, ambiguity persists in the definition of other social loss indicators, such as "missing people" or "affected people" that are still subject to relatively large ambiguities.

The information on actual economic losses remains difficult to compare. Although straightforward definitions exist for calculating direct physical impacts, such as affected buildings, agricultural assets and civil infrastructure, this is not consistently done for all disaster events across countries. Other losses are even less reported. These include indirect losses such as interruption of activities at business and household levels, transport interruption or interruption of lifelines or business activities. More intangible costs such as the impact on health or the environment are hardly ever accounted for due to difficulties in monetisation. As indirect and intangible losses are included to different extents, the comparability is not given. Economic losses are only reported for 30-40 percent of disaster events, and for those events where numbers exists, they can vary widely.

Gathering and comparing loss estimation methods of countries brings added value. The analyses of various damage estimation methods of countries and sharing them are useful exercises as this helps to design better estimation methods, with a clear focus to contribute to increasing the accuracy of existing disaster statistics. Coupled with actual loss assessment it is useful for countries to understand how they can conduct forward-looking ex-ante loss estimations, which can inform policy decisions especially on a project to project basis.

Collecting data on public (and private) expenditure for risk management is novel and could inform the assessment of the effectiveness of risk management policies. Systematic information on risk management expenditure, in combination with data on disaster losses would allow policy makers to evaluate whether risk management spending is effective in reducing the harmful impact of disasters. It would contribute to transparency and to promote risk management within countries. A common language to inform common approaches across countries in terms of risk management expenditure tracking would be valuable. The private sector would appreciate a method on risk expenditure as this would allow them to better assess the level of improvement in resilience against risks.

Tracking risk management expenditure has been established in a number of countries to promote a shift in investments from ex-post to ex-ante investments in risk reduction measures. The bulk of risk management funding still goes towards recovery and rehabilitation after disasters. Providing a full picture on where disaster spending flows helps to make the case for increased prevention and mitigation as well as preparedness funding. Additional motivators to collect such information were to ensure that level of investment is proportionate to risk, to ensure appropriate cost sharing arrangements, to demonstrate performance of risk management spending in reducing impacts in the long term.

However, expenditure information is not collected consistently. Very few countries systematically collect information on public (and private) expenditures. Australia, for example, collects this information regularly, but does so only for rehabilitation investments and not for overall risk management. In France, this has been done only for prevention investments. Physical infrastructure investments are widely included, but soft, non-structural investments in prevention are often not captured. The inclusion of private (e.g. HH and business) expenditure is more difficult – e.g. a questionnaire in France yielded little response. Analysing local budgets is important, but difficult to do without a proper mandate.

A common approach to accounting risk management expenditure is challenging. The countries that have collected such information have come across difficulties. In most countries there is no central repository (such as the national accounts) that clearly distinguishes and accounts for risk management. One challenge is therefore to identify all units that invest in risk management across sectors and levels of government. Depending on the administrative set-up of a country this exercise may be highly complex and requires research. Another challenge entails identifying “embedded” spending items, i.e. spending on a project that only partly contributes to risk management such as the meteorological office whose forecasting is a crucial element for early warning systems. The collection of such information is rarely mandatory, which makes it difficult for risk managers to extract such information across ministries and municipalities, as it has an administrative cost.

Annex B. OECD country survey and list of institutions of country responses

Direct and Indirect economic cost collection survey

The objective of the pre-filled Excel spreadsheet was to provide countries with a set of loss information that is available online. If this information is the official country information, all that countries needed to do was to confirm this to the Secretariat. Countries could alternatively correct and complement the information of the spreadsheet or send a different database all together. The spreadsheet was pre-filled with information available through EM-DAT or Desinventar, as well as, where relevant, information that was provided to the EU JRC initiative by some EU countries.

The Excel survey is based on a multi-hazard approach and includes data on hazard characteristics, fatalities, affected people, direct economic losses, physical losses and insured losses. In spatial terms, the survey requires disaster loss data to be reported at the lowest possible administrative unit, following OECD classifications (municipality or micro-region). The survey was designed to guide respondents by providing information in an accessible format. The spreadsheets included information on past disasters dating back to 1970, at least in those countries for which information was available since then. No thresholds in terms of disaster or impact levels were defined, in line with the Sendai Framework.

Table B.1. describes the set of variables collected through the OECD survey in relation to the Sendai targets.

Table B.1. Variables included in the 2016 OECD survey on the "Cost of Disasters

Category	Variable description
Event ID	This section includes general characteristics of a hazard event, a code for the geographic area where it took place, as well as dates when it took place: Event number: This is a unique identifier internal to the spreadsheet Geographic location ID: This is an OECD administrative code from the OECD regional database. This coding should make information across regions and OECD countries spatially comparable. The OECD has started to provide spatial codes if information on location that was provided was sufficiently specific. The Excel file provides the OECD codes for each country. Regions in OECD Member Countries have been classified according to two territorial levels (TL), to facilitate international comparability. The higher level (Territorial level 2) consists of macro regions, while the lower level (Territorial level 3) is composed of micro-regions. These levels are officially established, relatively stable and are used in most countries as a framework for implementing regional policies. Hazard code for main hazard type: This is based on the peril classifications found in the INSPIRE Natural Hazard Category[1] & IRDR (Institute for Risk & Disaster Reduction) peril Classification[2]. For storms the code ST was added to the list of codes and definitions and manmade hazard was replaced to anthropogenic hazard[3]. Date: Expressed as day/month/year when the observed event. In order to distinguish same types of events happening in the same year and in the same location, information of the day and month is preferred.
Hazard characteristics	This section complements the Event ID section with a more detailed classification of the type of hazard and potential sub-types. The columns "disaster types" and "sub-types" have been aligned as much as possible with the IRDR (Integrated Research on Disaster Risk) Peril Classification and Hazard Glossary (IRDR, 2015) as well as the INSPIRE Natural Hazard Category[4]. Name of geographic location: This is the precise location where the event happened. It is preferred to have event at the most disaggregated administrative unit Main hazard type: This is the main category of the event following the standard definitions. Hazard sub-type: This is more detailed information of the type of hazard.
Social losses – fatalities	Corresponding to Sendai Target A, this section contains figures for missing or deaths, separately. EM-DAT aggregates deaths, presumed dead and missing into the same figure. The Secretariat asked to provide this figure separate for missing and deaths in line with the Sendai framework.
Social losses – affected people	Corresponding to Sendai Target B, countries are asked to report how many people have been "directly affected". EM-DAT considers all people requiring immediate assistance during the emergency. Therefore, people reported injured or with houses being damaged or destroyed are also included. The Secretariat prefers to have information by subcategories in order to comply with Sendai definitions.
Direct economic losses	Corresponding to Sendai Target C, direct economic losses has been reported quite differently within countries (across different events) and across countries. At the moment, the UNISDR seeks to develop a standard methodology to harmonise future data collection for direct economic losses. For the OECD's purposes, it is important, for the time being, to have the direct economic loss figures reported by country and to understand what this includes. The direct economic losses should include public and private losses, including agricultural losses. On a side note: in EM-DAT, estimated damage is given in US$ thousands. For each disaster, the registered figure corresponds to the damage value at the moment of the event, i.e. the figures are shown true to the year of the event. Countries provided data in national currencies.
OECD physical losses	Adapted from Sendai Target D, this target will allow monitoring the total or partial destruction of physical assets existing in the affected areas. It is designed to monitor the damage to critical infrastructures and disruption of basic services. The collection of information on losses to physical assets can subsequently be used to calculate economic losses in a standardised manner. In addition to the indicators proposed by ISDR, the OECD establishes a broader definition of public infrastructure.

The complementary online survey collected information on countries' methods used for estimating economic losses, and on the responsibilities and criteria for collecting this information. Countries' responses together with desk research on economic losses provided the Secretariat with comparative evidence. In the online survey, countries were also asked to provide information on disaster risk management expenditures and on expressing interest in the development of an OECD framework to support the production of official statistics on economic losses.

Online survey

Instructions and survey

This short online questionnaire aims to build understanding of whether and how countries collect economic loss information and whether it informs risk management policy making. It complements the information collection survey on your country's social and economic disaster loss data. This information should help OECD understand how a standardised methodology could assist countries improve the collection of such information in the future.

The online questionnaire also asks whether disaster risk management expenditures are tracked in your country, and, if so, we would kindly request to have access to this information.

Part 1 – Contact details

[5] *Please provide your full name (first name followed by surname):

*Select your country:

*Name of the ministry/department or organisation you work for:

*Your job title:

*Your telephone number (may contain numeric values only):

Will only be used in case of follow-up/clarification question.

*Your email address:

Will only be used in case of follow-up/clarification question.

Part 2 – Economic loss data collection

*1. Is there a process by which your country has a ministry, agency or other government body that periodically collects data on economic losses (direct or indirect) from disasters?

a) Yes

b) No

c) Don't know

If No:

*1.1. What barriers prevent your country from collecting economic loss data?

If Yes:

*1.2. Who is responsible for collecting data on economic losses from disasters? I.e. The institution in charge of methods and instructions for carrying out data collection.

Please provide information on who is the lead organisation and who are the stakeholders involved in data collection and methods:

*1.3. Since when is such data recorded?

Please provide year or leave blank if you do not know.

*1.4. Does your country store economic loss data in a national, sub-national or sectoral repository?

a) Yes

b) No

c) Don't know

Please provide more details. I.e. Date of establishment, brief description, website and other pertinent information.

*1.5. What types of hazards are covered when your country collects economic loss data?

Please check all that apply.

a) Natural disasters

b) Man-made disasters

c) Don't Know

*1.6. Does your country have a threshold (such as a certain magnitude or number of people/places affected) that must be met before economic loss data is collected on a given event?

a) Yes

b) No

c) Don't know

If Yes:

1.6.1. Please describe the threshold and how it applies to loss data collection:

*1.7. Does your country separately account for direct and indirect economic costs?

a) Always

b) Sometimes

c) Never

d) Don't know

Please describe your country's methodology for collecting economic losses. If you prefer, please provide examples from 3 recent major disasters where economic loss information was collected:

*1.8. Does your country distinguish between publicly and privately accrued economic losses?

a) Yes

b) No

c) I don't know

Please provide more details. If you prefer, please provide examples from 3 recent major disasters where economic loss information was collected:

Part 3 – General information on disaster risk management and expenditures

*2. Do you use available international databases that report on social and economic losses (ex. EM-DAT, DesInventar) for disaster risk management?

a) Yes

b) No

c) I don't know

Please describe which international database(s) and how you use them:

*3. Do you anticipate that the development of an OECD framework to support the production of official statistics on economic loss would benefit your country?

a) Yes

b) No

c) Don't know

Please explain what you would expect from such a framework in order to benefit your country's efforts to collect such information in the future:

*4. Does your country collect information on Disaster Risk Management (DRM) expenditures?

a) Yes

b) No

c) Don't know

Please describe:

*5. How much did your country spend on DRM in 2013 (or most recent available year)? If recorded by your country, please provide information separately for ex-ante and ex-post expenditures.

Please provide details, including any links:

Note: The OECD is currently exploring data on national accounts, which could potentially provide us with estimates on civil protection budgets. We will try to exploit existing data as much as possible but would, for more granularities, be grateful to get DRM expenditure data, if available, from your country.

*6. Please indicate if you and/or another expert from your government would be interested in attending a meeting that could be organised to discuss the survey results and to explore how to further advance the effort to collect data on the socio-economic impacts of disasters.

a) Yes

b) No

c) I don't know

If the person interested in attending is someone other than yourself, please provide their contact information below or email Catherine.Gamper@oecd.org.

7. If there is anything you want to add to the questionnaire that you deem to be important to the subject but that you found to be insufficiently covered in this questionnaire, please add it here and/or send us any additional information through email.

Please describe:

Table B.2. Country respondents' institutions

Country	Name of the ministry/department or organisation
Australia	Attorney-General's Department
Austria	Federal Ministry of Agriculture, Forestry, Environment and Water
Canada	Public Safety Canada
Colombia	Planning Advisory Office - Ministry of Interior
Costa Rica	Ministry of Planning and Political Economy
Denmark	Danish Emergency Management Agency
Estonia	Ministry of Interior
Finland	Ministry of the Interior/Department for Rescue Services
France	Observatoire National des Risques Naturels (ONRN)
Israel	Central Bureau of Statistics ICBS
Japan	Japan Institute of Country-ology and Engineering
Mexico	National Disaster Prevention Centre
Norway	Directorate for Civil Protection (DSB)
Poland	Ministry of the Interior and Administration
Slovak Republic	Ministry Of Interior
Sweden	Swedish Civil Contingencies Agency
Turkey	Disaster and Emergency Management Authority

Notes

[5] * means the question was compulsory

ORGANISATION FOR ECONOMIC CO-OPERATION AND DEVELOPMENT

The OECD is a unique forum where governments work together to address the economic, social and environmental challenges of globalisation. The OECD is also at the forefront of efforts to understand and to help governments respond to new developments and concerns, such as corporate governance, the information economy and the challenges of an ageing population. The Organisation provides a setting where governments can compare policy experiences, seek answers to common problems, identify good practice and work to co-ordinate domestic and international policies.

The OECD member countries are: Australia, Austria, Belgium, Canada, Chile, the Czech Republic, Denmark, Estonia, Finland, France, Germany, Greece, Hungary, Iceland, Ireland, Israel, Italy, Japan, Korea, Latvia, Luxembourg, Mexico, the Netherlands, New Zealand, Norway, Poland, Portugal, the Slovak Republic, Slovenia, Spain, Sweden, Switzerland, Turkey, the United Kingdom and the United States. The European Union takes part in the work of the OECD.

OECD Publishing disseminates widely the results of the Organisation's statistics gathering and research on economic, social and environmental issues, as well as the conventions, guidelines and standards agreed by its members.

OECD PUBLISHING, 2, rue André-Pascal, 75775 PARIS CEDEX 16
(42 2018 27 1 P) ISBN 978-92-64-29873-6 – 2018

www.ingramcontent.com/pod-product-compliance
Lightning Source LLC
LaVergne TN
LVHW081414110826
845149LV00010B/1737

9789264298736